Soulmates with Paws, Hooves, and Wings

AMELIA KINKADE

2nd Edition

ISBN-10: 1482521156
ISBN-13: 978-1482521153

DEDICATION

To Mr. Jones, wherever you are in heaven or on earth, you are still the sunlight in my universe.

CONTENTS

ACKNOWLEDGMENTS

I'd like to thank my copy editor, Dr. Melinda McClanahan, without whose hawk-eyes many of the commas in this manuscript would have masqueraded as semi-colons and found themselves embarrassingly overdressed. Bless you, Mother, for pouring your loving attention over every word in this book. And I'm very grateful for my graphic designer, Rick Hupp, whom Mr. Jones secretly loved. (That's why he left the gift of "crystals" in his bed.) A big high-five to the team at Create Space who made this technology possible so that I could share these stories with the world. I'd also like to extend my heartfelt gratitude to every publishing house that turned down this book with the excuse that "anthologies don't sell." There's a saying, "Every kick's a boost." Thank you, publishers, for helping me boost this book up onto Amazon and allow it to land in the hands of those who will love and cherish these animals.

And most of all, I'd like to thank the real stars of this show: the contributors who let me tell their unforgettable stories. And I'd like to thank their owners for holding the pens.

FOREWORD: COMMUNICATING WITH ANIMALS
by Bernie Siegel, MD

We don't stop to think about how our animals reveal the fact that consciousness is non-local and that our chemistry is also detectable at a distance. Well known examples of this are dogs who can predict when their owners will have seizures or heart attacks, as well as, whether a mole on someone's leg is benign or a malignant melanoma. I hear many stories about pets who will not leave their sick owner's bedside and when they do show up in the kitchen for a snack the family knows the patient is getting better. I've seen this with our cat Miracle who doesn't check on me if I am sleeping late but if I do not get out of bed because I don't feel well, she is right there on my chest giving me a "purrfect" therapy session.

As far as consciousness is concerned it is obvious my animals know when I am thinking. They prove this to me every time I try to groom them, because that is the only time they all hide. When I change my mind and give up, they appear out of nowhere and suddenly, they are all underfoot.

I have learned a great deal from Amelia Kinkade and her books and work. We became friends out in San Francisco at a non-kill ASPCA conference. When she told me she was an animal intuitive, I was a non-believer but when I returned home and had a cat disappear, Amelia changed my mind.

I asked Amelia to find the lost cat and with no photograph or information, other than we live in the woods in Connecticut, one day an email came from Amelia detailing every single pet, garbage can, tree and more in the yard and saying the cat is alive. Amelia said she knew the cat was alive on earth because when she went outside to pray and locate the cat from her back yard in Los Angeles, she looked up at the full moon, praying under the night sky. Amelia then emailed me saying, "Booboo is alive! I can see the moon through her eyes."

The thing I couldn't understand was Amelia telling me the cat was under the house. It made no sense until the next

1

morning when I went out and after calling the cat's name , I heard her answer with a cry. She was under an outdoor stairway that came down to the ground on both sides. With food I enticed her out and rescued her.

Well if it works then I'll try it and learn from my experience. Amelia said you have to be calm in your head, not frantic, and get into the animal's head. So the next night I approached our bunny Smudge, who always runs around the yard and makes it hard for me to bring her in the house.

"Smudge, why don't you let me pick you up and bring you into the house?" Her answer blew my mind.

"You don't treat the cats that way."

I explained that the cats can handle themselves, but when it gets dark outside I didn't want any predator jumping the fence and attacking her. From that night on the problem was solved. Every now and then, she'd show her sense of humor by running around for a minute or two and we would both laugh.

One night, I'd been writing a story, which eventually became a book called *Buddy's Candle*, but when I first started the story, I took a break to take Furphy out for a walk. In the middle of our walk, out of nowhere, I "heard" a voice say, "Go to the animal shelter!" I acted on it, so we jumped in the car and headed down there. I walked in and asked the name of the dog sitting by the door. I was told his name was Buddy! The dog had just been dropped off by some lady who didn't like his behavior. I know why I was sent the message and home he came with us.

We stopped for gas and he leaped out of the car and ran out into the street and all the cars were stopping and people were trying to help me get Buddy back into my car. When we got home I asked him, "Why did you do that?"

He answered with I story I could never have dreamed of making up. "I lived with a couple. The wife was very nice but her husband was an alcoholic. When he would come home, she would ask him to take me for a walk. He would leave me in the car and go out drinking but then he would abuse me.

He hit me with sticks. When we got home he would lie to his wife about where we had been. So I don't feel safe getting into a car."

I explained to him I would never do that and that we were family and he had nothing to fear. I can still see that he gets nervous when I pick up a stick in the yard or a broom but it's not a major issue and with time he is no longer afraid of men with sticks.

The real test came two weeks later when a short time later I returned from shopping to find the sliding side door on the minivan open. I apparently had hit the button, accidentally, while putting the keys in my pocket. I couldn't believe my eyes. There sat Buddy in an open car. Furphy was missing and I started bellowing his name and running around until I was reminded of Amelia telling me to calm down and get into the dog's head. As soon as I did, I knew he was looking for me and probably inside the Stop and Shop with the manager yelling, "Whose dog is this?"

Sure enough, when I got to the door, the security guard asked me if I was looking for a dog. He had Furphy in his car with the air conditioning on where my dog was enjoying water and treats, just waiting for me.

Here is one last story for the disbelievers. I have taken our dogs to several of Amelia's workshops so they can be questioned by people who are learning the process. When Furphy and Buddy were new to our home they often urinated in the house. So my question to the class was why do they pee in the house so often. The answer I got was right on. "You have so many plants in your house they are confused about what's indoors and what's outdoors! | "

The next workshop was at the Omega conference center. At the lunch break Amelia and I and Furphy headed for the dining hall. I was told, "Dogs are not allowed in the dining hall." So I went in the back door and left Furphy sitting outside knowing he would wait for me to come out as he does at the bank, post office and wherever we go. A few minutes later a man came walking through the dining hall with Furphy in his arms, "Whose dog is this?" I acknowledged the problem was mine. He told me he had come in the front door. Everyone was impressed with Furphy's determination to be with me so he was granted permission to stay and have lunch with us.

In closing, let me say that as a physician, when I am caring for my animal under the direction of our veterinarian, I let them know that I am sorry that I have to do things to them that they are not happy about. I find they are more forgiving and less resistant to taking their medicine when I share my feelings with them.

Now Furphy does all the talking and I am constantly getting instructions on what to do all day so he is happy with our schedule. He is the alpha male but can't drive a car so he keeps me busy most of the day. When the car is quiet I know I forgot to let him jump in. He also insists I drive with one hand and pet him with the other while he occupies the front seat.

Do animals qualify as our Soulmates? If "Soulmate" means a doctor for your soul, and a good mate is a friend who can guide you through life, teaching you unconditional love every step of the way, who better than your animals can be your Soulmates? Enjoy these stories from people and animals all over the world who help us understand the meaning of true love, true healing, and a little bit of magic. Who better than our animals could teach us about life after death and everlasting love, too? Animals are complete and we have much to learn from them

Is Furphy my Soulmate? Well, best if you don't discuss it with my wife, but he does sleep with us and share meals so you decide...

A MESSAGE FROM THE EDITOR

People email me from all over the world and use my lingo. We are slowly creating a new technology in which to describe many indescribably states of mind. This thrills me. I chuckle to myself when one of my students writes, "Well, I sent him a Psychic Sandwich..." or "I sent him the Lumensilta and built the bridge of love..." because this is the only way I know that these instrumental ideas have become a real part of your lives. But the greatest compliment I've ever been given has not been the repetition of a phrase I made up. It is a phrase that my students coined, all over the world, simultaneously, mysteriously, without my help.

I mentioned in my first book about the love of my life, a little Maine Coon cat named Mr. Jones, and I dedicated the book to him with the words, "Wherever you are in heaven or on earth, you are the sunlight in my Universe." I didn't say much else about Mr. Jones, because Rodney was the star of *Horse's Mouth* and I didn't want to impinge on his territory. I told a few stories and I made a few indications that Mr. Jones was my sun, my moon, and my stars, but I tried to keep quiet about the intensity my feelings. I guess it didn't work.

The phenomenon started in Germany after I'd taught a workshop when one of my students came up to me and said, "Zee story about Mr. Jones and zee ants. It laughed me much!" She had flown all the way from Sweden. I leaned forward to hug her goodbye as our eyes filled with tears.

"It laughed me much, too, when it happened," I said, struggling to swallow the lump in my throat. This student and I happened to be leaving from the same train station so this quick good-bye was her only moment alone with me. This was all she wanted to say—nothing about me and nothing about what she had learned in the workshop. She just wanted to talk about Mr. Jones.

I took a breath and tried to steady myself. To think that only four years prior, I was scribbling in a notebook in the middle of the night, broke and downtrodden with no hope whatsoever of getting my crazy little stories published. I had been writing my private passions about a gray striped Maine Coon cat named Mr. Jones. Now a girl from Sweden knew his name.

The next day in Hamburg, a student came up after the workshop and singled out the same incident.

"The story about Mr. Jones and the ants! It so hard laughed me!" she said, giggling and crying and hugging me at the same time.

"Thank you! It so hard laughed me, too!" I said. No words or questions about the weekend, the process, her animals, my seminar, nothing, nada, zip. She just wanted to talk about Mr. Jones.

And three weeks later, the coordinator of my Scottish workshop came up to me and said secretively, "The story about wee Mr. Jones and all those cheeky wee ants—I've never laughed so hard."

Even from heaven, he maintains his celebrity status, kind of like Elvis. But more touching still is the meaning the name "Mr. Jones" has taken. I dry the tears of my students in Los Angeles, New York, Zurich, Glasgow, London, Paris, Johannesburg, Cape Town, Frankfurt, and Vienna, who not only know me and the name of my cats, they know my inmost secret: they know I had a "Mr. Jones," a four-legged love who was closer to me than my own heart-beat.

I'm still shocked when a stranger comes up to me in some foreign country, pulls out a photo and says in broken

English, "He is my Mr. Jones," or "She is my Mr. Jones," or worse yet, "I just lost my Mr. Jones."

I still can't hear his name without a chill rushing through me—my knees buckle and my eyes well up. At least once a week someone emails me from some obscure part of the world to say: "I just lost my Mr. Jones." How could this be? Every time I even read his name in print, it takes my breath. Some wild little book I wrote has coined a phrase internationally. "Mr. Jones" equals "love plus ten, times ten, squared." But, it's a secret love that no one else will understand, and to have "lost your Mr. Jones" means you just lost someone so precious that it defies all description, your partner in a cosmic relationship you're not supposed to talk about with other humans. The only thing that could blow my mind more than having people in Australia know the name of my cat, would be that they use his name as a metaphor for "love."

This analogy sprung into being in an array of languages all over the world. My students insisted that whether they speak German, French, Spanish, Norwegian or Korean, a "Mr. Jones" is a "Mr. Jones," and the one constant about the name "Mr. Jones" is that it has the same effect on everyone who utters it. It brings tears.

Well, I've been waiting for this moment. In this book, we're going to talk about healing—about how you can help heal animals and how animals heal you—but I can't do that without the assistance of my master teacher, so it's time to reveal to you my greatest secret. I need to tell you about Mr. Jones. Here's the story of how we met and what he meant to me. But don't tell anyone, okay? Because everyone will say I'm crazy.

1 MR. JONES: DANCIN' IN THE MOONLIGHT
By Amelia Kinkade

"Oh my God! Stop the car!" I screamed.

"Why?" my boyfriend argued.

"Just stop the car!"

"What is it, honey? Are you alright?"

"Just let me out! Did you see that CAT?" I was half way across the parking lot before his car rolled to a stop. We were on our way to a restaurant in North Hollywood.

"That's the most beautiful cat I've ever seen in my life!" I yelled over my shoulder, sprinting for the dumpster. When the cat saw me, running toward him like a madwoman, he took off down a brick wall. By the time I got there, only his gray fluffy tail was still in view as he ran for his life down the length of wall that surrounded the parking lot.

"Oh, wow," I whispered. "He's *wild.*" A shock of long gray stripes hung down over white paws. With his tail still held high like a feather duster, he stopped under a pine tree and whirled around to eye me curiously. Now from this safe distance, he could investigate the wild woman. That's the moment it happened. Our eyes met. Piercing green emeralds cut right through me. That was it.

"I've got to have that cat," I said.

By then, my boyfriend had parked and caught up with me, puffing. "Gosh, honey, I've never seen you run that fast in your life," he said with a chuckle.

9

"Look at him," I whispered. Never on God's green earth had I ever seen such eyes. Even my boyfriend gasped with wonder:

"Good Lord, he's beautiful. I think he's a Maine Coon." He didn't look like a house cat—more like a miniature lynx.

At this point in my life, fifteen years ago, I had already started a career as a professional animal communicator. Sending thoughts and pictures and receiving information from animals was old hat to me. I sent the thought, "Come up to me later and I'll give you some dinner. I'll be back."

Now, wouldn't you know, this wild cat was eating out of a dumpster behind one of L A's finest fish restaurants. He was no dummy. When I came out after dinner, I brought him a third of a piece of salmon is saffron sauce. Even as I lured him closer with the four star dinner—the sun was setting behind the stone wall throwing shadows on his fur—he didn't take it from me greedily. Fresh salmon was not a treat. He was used to it. Oh sure, he ate it, but he wouldn't let me get near enough to touch him that night...or the next...or the next.

It was on the fourth night that he finally let me pet him. I found him under a car in a pool of grease. Crusty cat food cans crawling with ants were scattered around the parking lot, so I knew some other people had noticed him. Every time a car engine started up in the parking lot, his body convulsed with a jolt, hair bristled like a porcupine. A shiver of pain ran through me as I thought of what his life had been like—living in a parking lot, hiding under parked cars, in the cold, in the rain. He wasn't a kitten. He'd already spent many years out here. I crouched under the car to lure him with a can of food. He came out when he saw me. As I reached for him, he performed an act I call "in-place biscuiting." That's when a cat marches in place, all four furry pistons kneading at the ground as they once did on their mother's breasts. There's no denying the state of bliss a cat's in when they "in-place biscuit." He tossed me a sly smile as if to say, "I really dig ya', babe. Just respect the fact that I'm *still wild*."

He was thin, straggly, nervous, and half-starved. As my fingers sank into his fur, I marveled at his long luxurious coat even after the hell he'd been through. His fur was like silk—his warmth like a magnet—if he were a well in the ground, I would have fallen in. I put a carrier in front of him and sent the thought of him walking into it without a struggle.

"Okay. Stop foolin' with me," I said. "Let's go home." I opened the door to the carrier and gave him a pat on the rump. He walked into it. I shut the door. And that was that. He was mine—or should I say, "I was his" from that moment on.

People often ask me how Mr. Jones got his name. (Over the years he became somewhat of a local celebrity.) The truth is, there was a cat in my old neighborhood who looked suspiciously like him named *Mrs.* Jones. I could never call out her name without laughing, so I named my new friend *Mr.* Jones.

Our love affair became epic—and irritating as hell to any human male in my life. At first Mr. Jones was an obsession who wouldn't let me touch him.

"Why are you so in love with that stupid wild cat?" they'd complain. "That mean cat! That grouchy old cat! He bites! He hisses! He sprays!"

My defense never made sense: "Not everyone you love has to come when you call them. No everyone you love has to slobber all over your face. He was *wild*. Give him a break!"

"He's still wild! And mean! And he throws up on my carpet. You'll never get near that damn cat." They didn't get it. I could worship him from a distance. As long as he wanted to live in my house, I was honored. That was all I asked of him. If I could feed him and look at him every day and adore him; if I could shelter him from rainstorms and cold nights, racing cars and ravenous coyotes; well, that was enough for me. But it wasn't enough for him.

It started in the garden. I'd take my notebook out back to write every morning after I meditated in the grass. One day I was meditating, eyes closed, and I felt a warm ball of fluff in my lap, trying to steady itself. That was his tactic. See, as long as I wasn't looking, he could sneak up on me. That made it his idea.

I had two other cats at home that Mr. Jones despised. He would never come near me when they were around. Because they slept on the bed, Mr. Jones didn't. Betty, my girl kitty got a massive crush on him—understandably so—and started ambushing him several times a day. Sometimes I'd catch her waiting to jump him from a chair high above. The minute he passed under the chair, she'd leap onto his back, standing up, paws rigid. For a split second, they'd look like one of those buses in London—a double-decker cat--before they went rolling in a whirlwind of spit and flying fur.

I'd urge her, "For Chrissakes, Betty, have some self-respect! I have a crush on him, too, but I don't attack him every time I see him." It never worked. She just couldn't contain herself. Did I blame her? Gosh, no. If I were a cat, I'd probably have made an ass out of myself over him, too. He had that effect on women.

Because Betty had claimed the bed, Jones boycotted it. I'd find him in the middle of the night sleeping alone downstairs on the couch. Finally, after two months, I couldn't stand the distance between us, so I took him up to the mountains for the weekend to be alone with me in the snow. Breakthrough. Alone and cold, he slept on the bed…with me. Odd things started happening.

Something occurred when we were alone together that winter that I've never told anyone. I'm going to let you in on my secret. I was lying on the couch with a fake fur coat draped over me. He jumped up onto my stomach for the very first time and began biscuiting the coat on my chest. Very relaxed, I let my mind float away, so joyous was I that he was finally beginning to bond with me. Suddenly, the energy shifted. He made himself weightless, so I could feel nothing but these marshmallow paws gently kneading me, and I drifted off into an alpha state.

In my meditation, the paws turned into hands. I have never been touched so gently in all my life. The heat of a thousand angels radiated out of these hands. I saw a vision of a man: gaunt, naked white skin with a shock of gray hair. Emerald eyes, keen as starlight, were staring into mine. He crouched over me tenderly caressing me with these healing hands, his warm breath on my throat. I screamed and sat up with a start! The little cat went flying.

"Oh my God! Who are you? *What* are you?" I yelled at him. By this point, he wasn't a man anymore, but a little disheveled house cat, shaken and trembling on the floor. What a vision! I had finally found a man who was quick, calm, confident, butch, madly in love with me and could summon enough healing energy to light up Manhattan—but he was a house cat. My luck.

As soon as we got home from our shamanic weekend together, he started boycotting the bed again. He simply couldn't tolerate my having other cats around me. But within the month, an event happened to change all that, and to further change my perception of what or whom was living in my house cat's body.

We were living in Los Angeles at the time, so if you were too, dear reader, you are no stranger to Mother Nature's impolite wake-up calls. I woke up in the middle of the night with my house on the hill swaying like a sailboat caught in a monsoon—6.9 in Studio City. A terror seized me that I had never felt before in my life. I flew out of bed and stumbled over something to the security of a doorway, wondering if the poles had shifted or if the earth had been suddenly thrown off its orbit. I went screaming into my boyfriend's arms.

When the tremor calmed, I did something really stupid, the last thing you are ever supposed to do in an earthquake. Seeing as how the power was off, I lit a match. Thank God, my house did not go up in a fireball as it might have if I had had a gas leak. A wave of reeling nausea hit me. What was it that I stumbled over? Everything I owned. The entire bedroom lay shattered on the floor. I was waist high in debris and spilled furniture.

There can be only a short lull between a warning quake and the one that's going to kill you, so my boyfriend and I shared a shocked poignant moment, wondering if we were ever going to see each other again. As I stood gasping with horror in the firelight at the shambles that was once my house, I only had two questions. The first was, "Are we going to die?" and the second was, "Where's Mr. Jones?"

I unearthed a flashlight and found Mr. Jones cowering under the guest room bed. I pulled him out by his ankles and scolded him.

"Look, you're coming with me! If I'm gonna die, I'm gonna die with you, and if you're gonna die, you're not going without me! Either we go together, or no one goes! Do you hear me?"

I put him in bed with me, but as usual he jumped off. In the wonderful world of Southern California, everyone knows that if the first tremor doesn't lead to a larger one, then that single tremor was the "big one," and will be followed by an aftershock.

I waited, and waited, and waited for an aftershock, but nothing happened. Seeing how it was 4 a.m. and there was nothing I could do to clean my house until daybreak, sans power, I went back to sleep. When it hit, I woke up screaming. It was no smaller than the first jolting roller coaster. The walls began to crumble around me. Clutching my rocking bed, I started praying out loud, desperately begging God to not let me die. Suddenly, I felt something warm and furry on my body. He pinned himself on my chest, spread eagle.

"I'm here, I'm here, I'm here! I'll save you, Amelia! If we're going to die, we're going to die together." If the ceiling should cave in and come crashing down on me, it would hit him first. At least he could shelter my heart, my lungs, and any vital organs his little body could cover. While every other house cat in Los Angeles was hiding under furniture seeking shelter, Mr. Jones was glued to my chest, convinced he could save me if my ceiling came crashing down. While every other cat in L A dove under, my furry cavalry dove *up*. He must have had to fight every survival instinct he ever had in order to risk his life for me.

Eventually, I moved out from that boyfriend's house and left the two other cats. I only took Mr. Jones. Rodney joined us six months later, and over time, he and Mr. Jones became great friends. But within our first few evenings alone together, Mr. Jones moved into my bed and onto my chest where he slept nightly for the next eight years. When I finally got a book on Maine Coon protocol, I discovered that Maine Coons are famous for picking only one human member of a family and bonding with that one person alone, often never letting the other members of the family touch them. This is why my boyfriends got the cold pad. I was the chosen one, and I became Mr. Jones's pet, his wife, his attendant, his possession—you know, just one of his things.

His glamorous face was the last vision I saw every night and the first I saw every morning. We did this kind of barrel dance all night. He always adjusted to stay on top. He would climb onto my chest and perch in front of my face, waiting for my eyelids to flutter. I woke every day in a spray of white whiskers, to see his emerald green eyes staring into mine. The minute I opened my eyes, a huge Cheshire cat smile spread across furry lips and a buzzing purr would vibrate through my body. In these dark years, I was battling a brutal depression problem, and I never wanted to come back to earth, so waking up was never fun for me. But the minute I saw Mr. Jones, I would think, "Ahh...you. Well, I guess if *you're* here, it's okay for me to be here, too." The only encouragement I had was seeing my own reflection in his adoring gaze.

In my care he flourished. Equal parts spun sugar and steel, Mr. Jones became solid muscle, in a coat as soft as a butterfly's belly. Tufts of fur sprouted out the bottom of his feet. I'd spend hours caressing the wisps of fluff between his toes. He had his own woodsy signature scent. Even after a scrub in the tub, Mr. Jones always smelled like a really expensive cigar. He was 100% male. All I had to do was bury my face in his fur and inhale that scent: every worry, every concern, every fear I ever had would unravel like a death shroud falling from my skin, to leave me standing radiant, shining, and young again. He could wash me clean.

Shortly after I left the first man, I got a new boyfriend. It took the new one about a month to be equally jealous of Mr. Jones. Here it came…again:

"You don't talk to *me* like that. You don't look at *me* like that."

A few months later, here came the haunting echo of the last ex-boyfriend's swansong. New man. Same old tune: "You don't love me as much as Mr. Jones!" It wasn't worth lying over.

"No, I don't, but you don't act like him, and if you did, I would. Now, go catch a rat, and take a crap in the back yard and leave me alone."

Mr. Jones never pestered me for attention. He never got on my nerves. If I were busy, he'd find something to occupy his mind, not tag around underfoot complaining that I was a bitch, a snob, a cold fish, or that I was just using him until something better came along. He was very low maintenance. We never fought over too much sex, not enough sex, too much money, not enough money, who was paying for what, who was giving more quality time to the relationship or who should have replaced the toilet paper.

He never complained about my cooking. I gave him fresh raw halibut, salmon, steak, and chicken. If he wanted something else, he'd go catch it himself.

Mr. Jones was not critical of me. He never told me I was too quiet, too moody, or too introverted; that writing is no way to make a living, or that no one out there wants to read about cats anyway.

He never made me throw dinner parties for people I didn't like. In fact, he'd object loudly if he caught me feeding neighborhood cats. He never told me to turn down the music and stop dancing around the living room. Mr. Jones, too, was always up for a little dancing in the moonlight. Every full moon, I'd let him stay out late, then together we'd dance around the coffee table while I sang to him:

"Dancin' in the moonlight. Everybody here is out of sight. They don't bark and they don't bite. It's a supernatural delight. Everybody's dancing in the moonlight..."

Nor did he ever call me "an old shrew" for preferring classical music to rap. To the contrary—my all-time favorite Chopin tune, Nocturne in E flat major, Opus 9 No. 2, was the only song I ever heard him sing along to. ("Rah-mreeee-mrah-me-rah-mrow.")

He never complained that I slept too late or forgot to do the dishes. And even when I did, he'd sleep on my chest if it meant all day and lick the dishes clean when we got up. He was always very helpful in the kitchen.

He never made me listen to endless boring diatribes about politics, taxes, homeless people, or illegal aliens. If anything homeless or alien wandered into our back yard, he would just catch it and eat it.

Mr. Jones never came home in a raging tantrum after a bad day at work to try to blame his problems on me. If a lizard or two got away, well, that was life. It certainly wasn't *my* fault. He'd pounce a little quicker the next day.

He never said things like, "You'll never make it in this world! You're too sensitive." "You can't really talk to animals. You're just psychotic." "You're sick all the time." "You're not really leaving the house wearing that?" And most importantly, he never said, "You're PMSing again!? Already!?" He didn't care if I wore black sequin lingerie or flannel pajamas to bed. He was ferocious only in my defense; endlessly protective, he never turned on me.

We didn't quibble over money. He wasn't cheap. If he was really hungry, he'd go out and catch two doves—one for me and one for him. If he was just moderately hungry, he's eat half a lizard and leave the other half for me. And often, when he wasn't hungry at all, he'd catch a mouse and give me the whole thing as a gift. He was generous to a fault.

He never whined, complained, or equivocated about his life. He wasn't wishy-washy. He was Clint Eastwood in fur, not Woody Allen. He never sat around fretting, "Should I catch this partridge? No, its eyes are too beady. Should I catch this sparrow? No, its feet are too scaly—" Pure masculinity in motion, he never apologized for getting what he wanted. Utterly uncompromising about his aggression, if he wanted something, he just took it. He never said he was sorry. He never made me spend Christmas with his mother, and best of all, in our eight years together, he never once turned on the television set.

I said to the new jealous boyfriend, "Listen pal, when you love *me* that much, maybe I'll love *you* that much."

Over the years people have often asked me if human spirits can incarnate in animal forms. I tell them no, it's rare, except for Mr. Jones...and then there was Travis.

I had a client, Janet, who has four gorgeous huskies. She had scheduled a house call for me to talk to her dogs. I made advance contact with the dogs through photographs, taking notes as I lay on my couch. Now, the first three dogs were dogs—bright smart loving dogs, but dogs, just the same. Then I connected with the fourth dog, Travis, a glorious white blue-eyed husky. As I slipped into a light trance, I suddenly felt strong human arms around me, rippling muscles pressed against my chest, lips on my neck, warm hands sliding down my spine.

"Uh, oh! This one's not a dog," I thought. Shocked and laughing, I tried to extricate myself from such a friendly introduction. I finally mustered the courage to finish my reading with Travis, but when it was over, I felt like I needed a cigarette. The minute I showed up at Janet's mountain home, Travis met me at the gate.

"Okay, you, I'm on to you! Don't try anything," I said under my breath.

Now, Janet's a wise old soul, a psychic herself and a musician; so I could tell her just about anything and she wouldn't balk that it was "too far out." I filled her in on the thoughts and feelings of her dogs. The dogs had seen her and nursed her and supported her though years of frustrating dating...especially Travis. The dogs had helped her heal psychically and emotionally from a bevy of childhood hurts...especially Travis. The dogs were her best friends, her playmates, and her spirit guides...especially Travis.

I tried to be tactful and not let the horse out of the barn when I said, "The other three dogs are like your children. You know, like they're dogs. But Travis isn't just your spirit guide. Travis is your husband."

Caught and surprised, she said, "So! You noticed!"

I just had to spill the beans. "Listen, Janet. I have something to tell you about Travis. Travis is..er, well...not a dog." She sat wide-eyed, mouth open. I took a breath.

"Travis is a man. A really sexy man." She leaned forward, and exploded with laughter. At last, there was someone with whom she could divulge her secret.

"I know!" she screamed. "Travis is a BIG SEXY MAN in a DOG-SUIT!"

After our discussion, I met Travis in the back yard. He didn't act like a dog. He didn't lick me or sniff me or do anything dog-like. He sauntered toward me, slowly scrutinizing me with this wicked come-hither gaze. Then he cornered me on a bench, standing up so we were eye to eye; he held his furry lips an inch in front of mine and stared me down with these crystal blue bedroom eyes. I didn't feel like I was meeting a dog. I felt like I was asking Mel Gibson to sign my T-shirt.

"Travis! Reeeally!" Janet roared.

"OK, Travis," I said, "I'm in love with you. You win! We all know how hot you are. Now, cut it out."

I found out over the years, that this was not such a rare phenomenon after all. When I started mentioning the morphing to a few of my most intuitive clients, I found that women all over the world were getting glimpses of their animal friends as humans. Don't worry. I'm not on my way to writing, *Animals as Teachers and Healers: And Psychic Sexual Surrogates*. And not all the animals present themselves as sexy men trying to jump their bones. One of my friends, Marty Meyer, an extraordinary animal communicator, says she regularly sees her dog as an old American Indian woman. When I met this old shaman dog, she revealed herself to me in this form, too, claiming to be Marty's spirit guide.

Even my old boyfriend who inherited Betty insisted she appeared to him in his meditations as a Japanese Goddess on a regular basis. Exceptionally intuitive, he woke in the middle of the night to a voice in his ear. The most scintillating little oriental woman was standing at his bedside, quietly whispering, "You are a wonderful man. Your work has great value. Your career will be highly successful—" He then realized Betty was asleep in his arms, purring. He had found his spirit guide. Many nights, she shape-shifted into her goddess form and appeared to him, quietly reprogramming his subconscious. That's why I had no guilt about leaving Betty in his care. She was his Mr. Jones.

I discovered another one of Jones's supernatural abilities by accident. Once when I had a pounding headache, I reached out to pet Mr. Jones. After a few strokes of his fur, my headache went away. The magic increased over the years. When I had a stomach ache, which was far too often, he'd appear out of nowhere, climb onto my stomach, and the pain would melt away. If I was feeling depressed, antsy or frustrated, I had only to touch his silky back and my emotional pain would be replaced by peace.

But there was more. Whenever I was really scared, bargaining with God in the middle of the night, and I made my usual threat, "If you can hear me, you'd better give me a sign," I'd feel the thud of little pads landing on the bed. He'd run to me and mount my chest, protectively massaging me with those white velvet paws. I'd hear his deep voice inside my head, "I'm here. I'm here. I'm here." This happened, not once or twice, but maybe once a month for eight years.

Shortly after I found him, like many sensitive people, I was an insomniac. At this time in my life, I was battling Post Traumatic Stress Disorder, and I'm afraid it was winning. When herbs and prayer or even wine couldn't even make me drowsy, that little cat would appear out of nowhere. The minute my hand settled into his resplendent fur, I'd fall fast asleep.

But then came the nightmares. Battling a hoard of demons, I'd wake up in the middle of the night crying, sweating, screaming, too terrified to go back to sleep—to find Mr. Jones had left the bed. The instant he heard me wake, he'd leap onto the bed, climb onto my chest, and take his silent vigil.

"I'm here, I'm here, I'm here!" Purring, he'd make himself weightless, and do the impossible. With an angelic energy that defied description, he'd put me back to sleep; then he'd accompany me into those dreams—soothing every hurt, caressing every scar, wiping away every tear, and championing me as we went to battle together against my memories. He was the only living being who could ever catch the reigns of the nightmares that had thundered through me like dark horses every night of my life. With only his presence, he could corral them, and create a quiet sanctuary inside me where I could sleep.

Little wonder, the human men in my life were so jealous. Throughout these years of hellish nights, I rarely called their names. It was only Mr. Jones who could enter the dark corridors in my mind to fill the frozen catacombs with warmth and light. He found nothing there too frightening to combat, nothing too monstrous to not overpower. He never shirked, he never cringed, he never said, "You're damaged goods. You're too fucked up. I can't handle it." When he found a hole in my psyche, he filled it. When he found shattered pieces, he fixed them. When he found wounds in me so raw and deep that no one else could touch, he healed them. Like a master surgeon at work—wordlessly, tirelessly—he cut and cleaned, sewed and salved, lanced and sutured. Effortlessly, he worked his magic. To him, the nightly surgery on my psyche was as easy as a piece of cake. He didn't resent it one bit.

Awash in the ecstasy of him, I was bathed in liquid light. Sometimes this light was not gentle with me. Often as he slept in my arms, as I drifted off to sleep, I'd almost get electrocuted. Bolts of lightning tore through him and rocketed into my body, sending us both bouncing in the air. Sometimes, I'd see the flash of lightening before it hit him. He'd fly in the air when it struck and I'd cry out when it hit me. Then, I'd dissolve into giggles as the energy dispersed throughout my body. It took me years to figure out what he was doing: He was ambushing my childhood demons, anchoring the frequency, using himself as a buffer, so that Spirit's healing energy could enter me no-holes-barred.

No amount of reasoning works as well as raw power. He did what no one else could do. He reached right into me and healed me. As the years went by, he appeased my panic and disarmed my invisible opponents. It took him years of tireless devotion to work his alchemy, but finally, finally, I could sleep peacefully and dream of snowy landscapes where we frolicked together in the early morning light. After eight years, he had finally corralled my stampeding nightmares and tamed my dark phantom horses.

Of course, there was another way that Mr. Jones sent my spirit soaring skyward. That darn cat could make me laugh until tears rolled down my cheeks. We'd have these photo sessions where I would pull out a really expensive camera. Mr. Jones would start posing for pictures like a super model on the runway, fans blowing, fur flying. I used to spend hours just gawking over his breath-taking beauty; but as soon as he saw the 35 mm come out, he would begin an aerobics routine of ridiculous poses, holding each pose for three seconds or so before going onto the next. Now, I'm not talking about an animal who was willing to patiently hold still for a few moments while you capture a shot or two. Mr. Jones would go through rigorous gymnastics, holding each contortion until he saw the flash, before changing position: Twisting, turning, arabesque, splits, pirouette, developé, grande jeté, on two feet, on his back, legs akimbo. *Flash! Freeze! Flash! Freeze!* These photo sessions could go on for twenty minutes. Like a soloist for Twyla Tharp's company, every modern pose was as interesting and dynamic as the last. Sometimes, I'd almost drop the camera I'd be so doubled over with laughter. These were the moments I lived for, and I have the scrapbooks to prove it.

As if these modeling sessions weren't hilarious enough, Mr. Jones found another way to enhance the photo shoots. He liked to balance stupid things on his head. Most cats are mortified by the idea of balancing toy halos or miniature reindeer antlers on their heads. They inch backwards, thrashing their heads and wriggling in disgust—but not Mr. Jones. He would prance and pose, careful not to topple the miniature top hat on his head. Put any stupid thing on his head and he would carefully balance it like a Chinese acrobat, all the while smiling and mugging for the camera. I thought this was a trait peculiar only to him, until I picked up one of those 365-cat-a-day calendars and found a plethora of proud photos featuring Maine Coons balancing stupid things on their heads. Most of the baby bonnets, devil's horns, Easter bunny ears, John Lennon glasses, and tiny witch's hats were photographed on the heads of smirking Maine Coons. Mr. Jones could even follow a evening photo shoot by showing up for dinner formally dressed. He could eat an entire bowl of food without spilling his top hat. Mr. Jones had class.

Every time I called him, he came running, meowing up at me as he trotted along. Never once, not once in our life together did he not come when I called. I never even had to run the can opener. Each time he came to my call, chattering, "I'm coming. I'm coming," it would always make me laugh. Every day when I left the house, he would wait for my return on the front door step; then, he'd run up to my car and climb in my open car door. He'd walk me to the door, chattering and telling me about his day. I called him my "valet" and roared with laughter. Once, when I wasn't home, a boyfriend witnessed him leap up out of a dead sleep, run to the front door and chatter desperately to be let out.

Ten minutes later the boyfriend heard my car pulling up into the driveway. Mr. Jones trotted over to greet me and climbed in my car door. This even impressed my most skeptical boyfriend. *Dogs Who Know When Their Owners Are Coming Home*, pshaw! That book should have been titled, *CATS Who Know When Their Owners Are Coming Home*. This cracked me up because Mr. Jones proved his point to his astonished nemesis, as if to say, "You claim I can't talk to her, and you didn't even know she was on her way home, you *idiot!*"

There was another incident that I can't even recall without slapping my thigh and laughing out loud, and this one involved a trick he played on this same boyfriend, Rick. I had two human relationships during my eight-year marriage to Mr. Jones, and Mr. Jones had the same attitude toward both men. Even though he lived with them both—one for four years and one for three—he never said anything to either of them except, "Don't touch my wife!" and "Get out of my house!"

Of course, they both had to at least feign love for him so they tried to appease him. To please me, Mr. Jones pretended to tolerate them. This meant, in his most benevolent moments, he would allow them to pet him for about thirty seconds before he bit them and growled, "Don't touch my wife!" and "Get out of my house!" In all honesty, both men fell secretly in love with him, and as long as I wasn't watching, they'd have covert petting sessions. But the instant I walked into the room and caught them red-handed, Mr. Jones would jump up, alarmed and embarrassed. He'd hiss wildly and the men would curse: "Mean old Mr. Jones!"

Rick loved to harass him. He would pet him too long and allow himself to get bitten—even with Mr. Jones growling "badarbarbahdagrahab"—and then Rick would chase Mr. Jones all over the house. One night, I guess the pestering took its toll.

I'm a Capricorn and very attached to all kinds of rocks. I sleep with crystals in my hands every night—rose quartz, lapis, citrine, tourmaline, but my bed ends up looking like a rock quarry after I've dropped them and tossed them around all night. The rocks go where I go, so both men loved to bitch about my turning their beds into a box of rocks.

Well, this night after Rick, the insufferable pest, had really made a nuisance of himself and thoroughly irritated Mr. Jones, Mr. Jones decided to express his sentiments—in Rick's bed. Either Mr. Jones was very dehydrated that day, or he had left his sentiments earlier that day, so by the middle of the night, his expression of discontent was as hard as one of my "damn crystals."

To make matters worse, Rick was germ-phobic and squeamish about litter boxes, with the world's most sensitive nose, and he enjoyed nothing more than complaining about my very best perfume. We weren't living together yet, but sharing time between two apartments, and of course I took Mr. Jones with me to and fro. After Mr. Jones and I left, when Rick finally stumbled into bed, too tired to even flip on the light, he found that I had left a pile of my "damn crystals" under his pillow—until he picked one up in his squeamish little hand and held it up to his ultra-sensitive snout. Well, you get the picture.

When I got the angry call the next day, "Do you know what mean-old-Mr. Jones did to me last night!?" even the pest couldn't stop laughing. Rick knew he had deserved it. Mr. Jones had finally settled the score.

But there were more idiosyncrasies that made mean ol' Mr. Jones extraordinary, and some were not even supernatural, but naturally super. When I first started studying animal communication, I was still working as a professional jazz dancer. As all my dancer friends heard that I could talk to animals, they'd shake their heads, roll their eyes heavenward and mutter, "yeah, right." Some of them had even heard through the grapevine that my cats could speak English out loud, not telepathically, but literally, verbally, enunciating English words. I'm sure my friends would give each other knowing looks behind my back, wink, and tap their foreheads, saying, "Yes, but we all know Amelia is a little... (tap, tap, tap)" One of the most skeptical of the group was a gorgeous girl named Scott, who had heard me mention that Rodney could "talk." I'll never forget the day Scott sat in the den with me, sipping a hot cup of tea, when Rodney yelled from the other room: "MOM! AHWANNOUT!"

Scott flew off the couch screaming, "Amelia! There's a baby in your living room!"

"That's only Rodney," I said smugly. "I told you Rodney could talk."

"MOOOHM! I WANNNNOUT!" he hollered.

"I'm coming," I yelled back. Scott was white as a ghost. I met him in the living room where he stood waiting impatiently for me to open the sliding glass door. Scott looked on, astonished. This was routine for Rodney and me. Eventually, he even took it further. One day, after I opened the door and he trotted out, he stopped and coolly looked over his shoulder at me.

"Fanx!" he said.

Mr. Jones never strung together elaborate nouns and verbs. He only spoke one English word, but it was a tongue twister for a little cat. He never called me "Mom," like Rodney and all my other cats did. I was his wife, not his mother. Whenever he greeted me, he'd look up at me with the most profound look of love in his eyes and say, "Me-la," "A-me-ra," "A-me-ri-a." After years of practice, he learned to enunciate. Sometimes, he'd get it right on the nose: "A-me-li-a! A-me-li-a!" I'd grab him, explode with laughter, and we'd roll around on the floor.

Wherever I found Mr. Jones outside in the back yard, I found hummingbirds orbiting around his head like satellites.

They would swoop down on his head and hover, "Good morning, Mr. Jones!" They were very polite. He would look up at them and grin. The stealth bomber of cats, Mr. Jones was a well-oiled killing machine, but he never even took a swat at his hummingbirds. He knew his limitations. Every morning, they hovered six inches above his whiskers, whispering sweet nothings in his ears, taking advice from the godfather of the hummingbird mafia. All day, they'd circle his head like the moons of Saturn. How could I blame them? I had gotten sucked into his gravitational field, too, orbiting him like one of his many moons. Spinning above his crown chakra, as if on invisible antennae, the tiny whiz-kids were irresistibly attracted to him. I can only assume that because these minuscule birds vibrate on such high frequencies themselves, that they, like me, were addicted to his heavenly shaman energy. *Yum. Yum. Buzz. Buzz. 'Can't get enough.* Mr. Jones's hummingbird halo always made me laugh.

Unfortunately, we had to leave the house with the big back yard and with it, the avatar's buzzing bird crown, to relocate to a small apartment. By this time, Mr. Jones was getting older and not as capable of defending himself with his signature Clint Eastwoodesque whoop-ass savoir faire. A neighbor's cat, Mishka, had already established dominance in our courtyard, and within days, Mishka was beating the tar and the pride out of my prize boxer, Mr. Jones. It broke my heart (and almost my eardrums) to witness these howling harrowing cat fights and see him take his daily beating. I wasn't about to have my hero play second fiddle to some punk of a cat off the street, but I didn't know what on earth to do to restore my old man's dignity. As fate would have it, the lion angels must have been listening, because I took a pilgrimage up to Shambala, Tippi Hedrin's big cat sanctuary, a rescue facility North of Los Angeles that houses an array of enormous wild cats. I happened upon the lions just as their keeper was brushing them, so I confiscated a big clump of lion hair from the keeper's comb and smuggled it into my pants pocket all the way home to my new apartment. If you haven't had the pleasure of inhaling lion hair first-hand, let me assure you, it reeks to high heaven, and the scent is so gamy, it sends you reeling with what I call 'ode de musky smelling funk.' I evenly distributed the lion hair in the herb garden on the balcony where Mr. Jones was trying to establish territory. Once I hid the aromatic feline skunk potion in the garden and Mishka got the idea that there was a five hundred pound lion in our apartment, he left Mr. Jones alone for quite a while.

It was in this busy apartment building in Studio City where the little shmoozer began building a secret fan club. The resplendent Mr. Jones would sit on his balcony, tending his herb garden, charming all the neighbors. When none of my neighbor's knew I was home, I'd creep out on the balcony and eavesdrop. Nothing tickled me more than to hear my neighbors as they passed by. I'd chuckle to myself when even the men stopped to coo, "Good morning, Mr. Jones." "Howsit going, Mr. Jones?" "Whassup, Mr. Jones?" "Don't you look handsome today, Mr. Jones?!" Over time, Mr. Jones's fame helped me separated my close friends from my acquaintances. When my acquaintances called me on the phone, they'd ask, "How are you, Amelia?" But when my best friends called, they'd cut me off and joke, "Well enough about you. How's *Mr. Jones?*"

They sensed something divine in him. And their suspicions were right. Mr. Jones launched me beyond his naturally super level and even beyond his super natural level into a level of intuitive awareness that I never dreamed possible. Clairvoyance and Clairsentience ('clear-seeing' and 'clear-feeling' in Latin) are by far the most common psychic gifts that one develops when one first learns interspecies communication. Although my knack from the start was Clairaudience, (clear-hearing' in Latin, the ability to interpret intuitive information into words) no one could have honed it, pushed me, and sharpened my skills on a daily basis better than Mr. Jones. He taught me how to listen consistently, to hold a frequency so high, it was almost painful. It took every ounce of concentration I had to access his frequency. But I loved him so much, I couldn't help but raise my vibratory rate to match his. It was the only way we could be together.

Under his tutelage, I was profiled in a book called *The One Hundred Top Psychics in America* (Simon and Shuster) that sent my private practice soaring into the stratosphere at warp speed. Inundated with highly emotional clients who relied on me, I found myself discussing my other animal cases with Mr. Jones. I discovered he could convey information to me about their medical and behavioral problems with more clarity than I could glean on my own. I've explained to a few of my clients who own these "special" animals that there are psychics in the animal realm as well as psychics in the human realm. When I couldn't get a solid answer about the needs of one of my clients, I would just ask Mr. Jones. He could pick up where my ability left off. In my last book, *The Language of Miracles,* (New World Library) an astronaut named Dr. Edgar Mitchell and I used the model of the Quantum Entanglement to describe how one energetic field might respond and react to all the other energetic fields around it, suggesting that each living being resonating within the constellation is sensitive to the holographic quantum information (the thoughts, the feelings, the physical sensations) contained in each member of the group. I know it sounds heady, but in more simple terms, Laura Day, the famous intuition teacher says, "How do you know the difference between psychic and psychotic? If you're psychic, your information is *right!*"

Jones was always right. If he told me a dog's tumor was not cancerous, when that dog went into surgery to have in removed, his vet would find that it was not cancerous. If Jones said a cat was about to die, sure enough, that cat would cross over when predicted. Talking to Jones was not like telepathing with any other animal. Talking to Jones was like having a direct phone line to God. Sometimes, though, he had his own personal agenda.

I'll quickly recant the Ant Story that became the most popular anecdote in my first book, *Straight From the Horse's*

Mouth: How to Talk to Animals and Get Answers (New World Library), just in case you're wondering what the hay I was ranting about in the prologue. When I was living alone with Mr. Jones in my apartment at Venice Beach, I had to spend a lot of my time working in the San Fernando Valley. The Valley is approximately thirty minutes away from the beach, and at least an hour and a half away in five o'clock traffic, which was exactly the time I had to go over the hill every other day.

During this time away, I kept close psychic tabs on Mr. Jones, mentally checking in on him several times a day. He had a cat-door enabling him to explore the neighborhood, so we made an agreement that he would meet me inside every night. Even though my arrival times varied from day to day, he was never more than five minutes late getting home. Our communication was impeccable. He never let me down. So when I got this urgent communication one afternoon, I knew enough to take it seriously.

I was trapped on the Northbound 405 freeway in five o'clock traffic when Mr. Jones blasted into my mind. This alone was unprecedented. I usually have to initiate communication with absent animals, even with my own cats—the animals rarely speak first—but this message interrupted my thought process like an emergency broadcast on the radio.

"Amelia, COME HOME." A wave of panic shot up my spine. "What is it? What is it?" I asked.

"Something terrible is in the house! COME HOME NOW!" "What's in the house? Tell me who it is!" I begged. "INVADERS! COME HOME! JUST COME BACK HOME!" Mr. Jones implored. I didn't wait to find out who was in the house. I blazed off the freeway at the next off ramp. Making a U-turn, I sped back to the apartment. What was it? Robbers! I fretted. It felt like robbers.

I hurled the command to Mr. Jones: "Run out your cat door! Don't let anything stop you! Run outside right now and wait for me!"

When I got there, the building wasn't on fire. The windows weren't broken, the doors weren't bashed in. Everything looked utterly copacetic. I crept up the landing with a can of pepper spray in my hand. There I found Mr. Jones waiting for me on the front doorstep, purring contentedly enough, but stiff on his feet, looking a bit disheveled.

"What is it?" I whispered. "You scared the daylights out of me!"

When I was certain I could hear no one inside the apartment, I unlocked the door and let us both in. As my vision adjusted to the dim indoor lighting before I saw the treacherous intruders.

ANTS! A line of ants marched from the sliding glass door all the way into the kitchen where they were playing King of the Hill on Mr. Jones's food bowl. His food was absolutely black with crawling ants. Pieces of dry food were being passed from one jaw to the next, assembly line fashion, and spirited out the crack in the sliding glass door. What could be more tragic to a cat, than to have his food confiscated before dinner time? I laughed with relief and thanked him for his mind-blowing communication skills before I gave him a fresh bowl of food.

"Gosh, Jones, why didn't you just eat them?" I asked him. (He sometimes likes to snack on ants.)

"Too many," he said.

There was another time he initiated a conversation that really blew my mind. He often slept on the front doorstep under a yellow rose bush. Sometimes the bush would become so laden with blossoms, the roses would drape down and touch him. I stepped outside to find him lying with a giant yellow blossom on his back, just weeks before I got my new bedspread. When he jumped onto my new bright yellow bedspread, he sniffed around and nosed at one of the yellow hibiscus printed on the comforter. Then, he started in-place biscuiting it and smiling up at me with that irresistible white furry overbite.

"I like it," he said. "We have the same taste." With this, he sent me one of the most vivid images I've ever received from an animal. It was of the yellow roses he lay under. I had never thought of them as his bedspread before, but as his eyes twinkled up at me, I realized he wasn't just offering up a comparison. He was making a joke.

But one of our most revealing conversations was about his origins. I asked him how he came to be in that parking lot behind that fish restaurant. His answer brought tears to my eyes. He had walked very far across a dangerous part of town to arrive at that spot. Tired, scared, hungry, dodging cars, he had made a long trek—but he had not made it alone. He showed me two "white people," two tall white human spirits flanking him, protecting him, guiding his every step. They directed him to the parking lot and waited with him until I eventually showed up.

"But, how did you know where to find me?" I asked.

"They told me: If you wait here, she will come."

I did. But I wish I had come sooner. Mr. Jones was already past him prime when we first met, but once his kidneys started to fail, I found myself on a downward spiral. His nausea was out of control. At one point, one genius vet told me he had three months to live without daily injections of fluids. Because Mr. Jones and I had agreed he would never be subject to daily injections, I was trying to find an institution in which to commit myself; then I found a better vet.

A second opinion revealed nothing more than a chronic flea allergy, making him throw up six times a day. He, like his mother, was overly sensitive and allergic to everything. I put him on Frontline and a cure-all herb called Una Gato. (Cat's Claw) I funneled healing energy into him with my hands. Once we got his problem under control, he put on weight and lived another two and a half years thriving on fresh steak, fresh salmon, and fresh swordfish. He became a crotchety old man, mean and grumpy—but alive. Maybe my threat, "You're not going without me," kept him going for longer than it should have.

As he slowed down, I slowed down. As he became more incapacitated, I became more incapacitated. In the very end, when he was blind in one eye, on high blood pressure medication, and had lost his ability to jump, to run, to walk, and finally to stand, I was an inconsolable wreck, bursting into tears in public places and fantasizing about different methods of suicide. This was the only arena in which our telepathic communication ever broke down. No matter how much I obsessed over his health problems, fussed over his medications and supplements, and desperately begged him to tell me how to heal him, he would never give me one scrap of information about his medical condition. His response remained the same:

"Don't worry your pretty little head."

He had offered up the promise that he would stay until I finished my first book, *Straight From the Horse's Mouth*. He claimed he was helping me write it, and since he jumped in my lap every time I began to write, bringing with him a burst of inspiration, I knew that this was true. He was my meowing muse. I wrote like a mad fiend those first two years, but as I started nearing the end of the book, I started stalling. Whatever I did, I just couldn't stop revising the manuscript. Even when he was almost completely blind, refusing to eat, refusing to move, I kept saying, "It's not finished. It's not good enough. You can't leave me here without you. I'm not ready! I'm not ready!" My life became a constant prayer: "Please God, please don't take him, please don't take him, please God...not yet."

I spent those last two and a half years getting ready for the inevitable and ironically enough, counseling and comforting all my clients as their animal friends departed this world. I assured them that death was an illusion, that their animal spirits live on forever, that the passage was freeing and joyous, that the Other Side is a blissful replica of their happiest moments on earth. I negotiated times of death with their animals. I negotiated terms of death with their animals. I asked their animal if they needed medical assistance or if they could go on their own. I helped them set up signals so that they could let their guardians know when they were ready. I even channeled them from the Other Side to give messages to their guardians about their wellbeing and whereabouts.   I was like an unshakable pillar of comfort, assuring the humans that the animals would go only when they're owners were ready—only when their guardians were strong enough to let them go. I was a 24-hour-rest station for the weary and frightened, calming their fears and infusing them with peace. But I never let my clients in on what I was really feeling. I carefully squelched the voice inside me that droned on endlessly for almost three years: "Please God, please don't take him, please don't take him, please God, no—not yet!" I had a chronic case of "the cobbler's kids have no shoes."

In the very end, when he was howling at things I couldn't see, barely able to move, but still insisting that he did not want the interference of euthanasia (He was too proud for that), I asked my departed Grandmother, Rheua Nell, to take him. She keeps all my cats. I had hung a framed picture of Rheau Nell on the wall in my bathroom. On a Sunday night, in the middle of the night, Mr. Jones bolted up and in a delirious run, threw himself through the bathroom door and started letting out piteous howls. Bolting into the room to see what was wrong, I found him howling at my Grandmother's picture. Rheau Nell had come for him.

How did we live through that night? I don't know. He had always insisted he could go on his own. He loathed vets. Fortunately, only months before his death, we found Dr. Karen Martin, a vet in Los Angeles who has the magic touch with cats. She was better with Mr. Jones than anyone on the face of the earth. Not only did he refrain from trying to bite one of her fingers off, as he had done with all his prior vets, when she first touched him, he purred. My eyes filled with tears at the miracle. But when her eyes filled with tears, too, I knew we had found our new vet. As she put acupuncture needles in him, he revved his engine and made googoo eyes at her. Utterly smitten, he agreed that if he should ever need assistance saying his good-byes, Karen was the one to do it.

Suddenly one day, Mr. Jones stopped eating. Rather than encouraging him to leave peacefully as I had advised all my clients for so many years, I was prone to out-of-control tantrums. Like a hysterical three-year-old, I'd throw myself at his feet and scream, "I won't live without you! I WON'T! I WON'T!!!" Little wonder the little guy had such a tough time leaving me.

If there's one drawback to being an Animal Communicator, it's having people sobbing like hysterical freaks, calling you all hours of the day and night. I've always complained about it. My friend, Marty Meyer, is a Class-A Animal Communicator, so what did I do? I called Marty, sobbing like a hysterical freak, begging her to tell me if Mr. Jones wanted to be put down. Her answer will make me smile for the rest of my life. In the same crotchety deep tone I knew to be his, she translated for him:

"He says he won't go! He says he wants to stay with his wife. (me) He says, "No. I like my life the way it is." I looked down at him, and started to laugh like a lunatic through my sobs, "But you're blind, and you're starving, and you can't stand up! You stubborn old asshole! There's nothing left of you! You're a wraith! You've got to go!"

But I couldn't let him go. Not yet. Mr. Jones and I spent four days together before his ascension. I never left his side. There were conversations that transpired in those wee hours of the night; granted, I was sleep deprived, punchy from crying, and delirious with pain, but there were new things—magical things—that I'd never experienced before. During our last night together, as I pet Mr. Jones, blue lights bounced out of the top of his head like fireworks. My hand became transparent and I could see through it as if it weren't even there. As he started turning into pure electric energy, my body began to dissolve. I had to make a decision that night. Was I going to go with him? Could I let him go without me? Was life worth living without him?

As he lay beside me, the plot ending to *The Winged One*, a children's novel was revealed to me. I'd been struggling with the story for years and could never get the ending right. Now, out of the blue, I saw every detail of how the book should end. The plot twist absolutely took my breath. Quickly, he summarized it for me. I guess he wasn't going to be around to help me write it, so he had to give me the short version.

And finally, and most astonishing, at 4 a.m., he appeared to me in human form and gave me a lecture. He showed me himself as part of the council of angels that govern this planet. He explained who he really was, why he'd come, and what I'd come to earth to accomplish. He told me where we'd met and how ancient our relationship really was. He said he was sorry he had had to take the form of a little cat. He said he was sorry his life span was so short and that the little body had finally given out. He said it had been the only way to get to me—that he would have done anything to be with me. He assured me that he'd never leave me, but join forces with me. They had agreed he could infuse my body with his energy from the Other Side.

Then, he showed me a scenario and gave me a single piece of advice I will remember for all time. He showed me the two of us in human form, performing surgery side-by-side amongst a circle of doctors. I saw a sponge soaking up blood, then a knife cutting away a tumor.

"Sponges heal, Amelia," he said, volleying an image of myself absorbing all the pain and negativity from my clients, leaving them healed and myself holding the bag.

"But so do knives." With this, I saw a knife in his hand, making a clean incision and taking with it none of the diseased tissue it sliced away. The knife gleamed, silver and untouched. The blood dripped straight off.

"Right now, you are a sponge. You've got to learn to be a knife. If you don't learn to be a knife, they're going to kill you. You're going to die." I promised to work on it. He promised to help me.

The next morning, he was barely alive. When I asked him if he wanted to go visit pretty Karen, he finally gave his consent.

I clipped a sumptuous bouquet of yellow roses from his garden and took them with us. I placed the bouquet of roses in front of his eyes so that the buttery petals would be the last thing he ever saw. Karen brought a candle in. Its flame sputtered, almost extinguished by a teardrop streaming down her cheek. She gave him a sedative to knock him out before she put the needle in.

I love you. I love you. I love you.

After we got into the car, and were halfway home, Rick my boyfriend who drove us, stopped for gas. This was the boyfriend who had received the gift of Mr. Jones's "crystals," and even he couldn't stop crying. I was clutching Mr. Jones, my lips pressing against his head, my tears soaking him like summer rain. I let the ocean of agony pour through me, trying to let go, but I didn't feel he was spiritually dead. Although he was technically dead—his heart had stopped beating and Karen had pronounced him dead—I hadn't seen his spirit leave his body, and as I hugged him to my chest, I felt his presence still in the "dead" body.

When Rick left the car, I noticed one of Mr. Jones's eyes was still open, so I tried to poke it shut with my finger. He let out a loud "merrooowww!"

I screamed and surprised myself with a peal of laughter. "For heaven's sake, Jones!" I said. "GET OUT OF THAT BODY! You're supposed to be *dead!*"

Even in a dead body, he could perform supernatural feats. When we returned home, I lay him on his bed in the middle of the living room floor, in a circle of roses and photographs of our eight years together. He still had not left his body. Out of the corner of my eye, I thought I caught him moving.

Utterly heart-broken and inconsolable, I did something I
rarely do—I switched on the radio.

This is what I heard:

"Lying here alone I'm dreaming,
My mind keeps wandering.
My thought are only you,
wandering through the memories of my mind.
How could love so real have turned so empty?
I just keep wandering why.
Will I ever find the love we shared together you and I?
It's you, sweet baby,
Though we've had such a long hard road to climb,
sweet baby.
Only hopin' it's not too late to try again.
It's you, sweet baby. I will never be free from your
embrace.
Sweet baby, won't you try to believe in what I say?
I will always be right there by your side…right by your
side."

Call me superstitious for thinking Spirit can speak to us
through lyrics of songs, but if not through music—how? The
next day, he finally left his body, and the next day, I buried
him under a baby apple tree. One of my dearest students and
oldest friends sent a generous bouquet of flowers. She knew
nothing of the apple tree. When I looked closely at the
bouquet, I saw that the huge round vase was filled with
something unusual. I looked closer. What was submerged in
the vase? Baby apples.

"Denise," I asked later, "why on earth did you have
the vase filled with apples?"

"I don't know," she said. "I just wanted to do
something special. I needed a symbol to represent eternal
life." I smiled at the thought of the little Maine Coon

whispering on her shoulder when she picked up the phone to call the florist.

"Tell them to fill it with apples. Baby apples. She'll understand."

A week later, on the anniversary of his death, I turned on the radio, wondering if I would ever hear that song again. The instant I touched the dial, it had already begun: *"Lying here alone I'm dreaming, my mind keeps wandering. My thoughts are only you..."*

Later that day, at three o'clock, the time of his departure, I found myself in a drug store. Our other theme songs wafted overhead: *"Dancin' in the moonlight. Everybody here is out of sight. They don't bark and they don't bite. It's a supernatural delight. Everybody's dancing in the moonlight..."* It was the song I used to sing as we danced around the coffee table.

As I stood frozen, weeping uncontrollably in the isle, a woman's voice came over the intercom interrupting the song: "MR. JONES! MR. JONES! You're wanted on line 233!" One of my favorite sayings is, "Synchronicity is God's way of remaining anonymous." Never was this more true.

When I visited Marty, and asked her to translate for him from the Other Side, she had no trouble contacting him. He told her he was relieved to be out of that body. It had been very limiting for him to try to contain all his energy in the body of a little cat, but he was willing to do it only for me— that he would have done anything to be with me. He would have taken any form just to get close to me. She saw him in human form now, ricocheting back and forth from the cat he once was to a big man, dressed in white. Then, she confirmed the impossible:

"He says he can help you now more than ever from where he is. He says he's not going to leave you, but channel his energy into you. He says he's the gatekeeper between heaven and earth. He says he's part of a council now—"

"Really, Marty, how often do dead animals tell you they're part of the Great White Council? Have you ever heard that before?" I asked incredulously.

"Well, no. Their spirits are usually just animals like they were on earth."

So, I let Marty in on my secret, and now, I have to admit I've been withholding information from you, too. There's more to my little secret.

You see, when Mr. Jones appeared to me in human form, he had…wings.

When No One Calls "Last Dance."

The years have slipped by and as I fly all over the world lecturing and wearing myself out, Mr. Jones makes his presence known in shockingly beautiful ways. Last year, I was teaching on the Isle of Man en route from Scotland but I had been having a particularly difficult trip. Moody, jet-lagged, weepy, and sick, I dragged myself through the Glasgow airport worried I'd miss my flight. Usually touring and teaching is a delight for me, but I've never stopped missing Mr. Jones. This trip, I had the flu and a bad case of the poor-mes. I found myself staring at a magazine in a snack shop that had a promotional CD sealed under the plastic. The CD was nothing I was interested in. It was a compilation of dance music called "Party Starter." God knows, the last thing I felt like doing was dancing. I thought it was odd, though, that a woman's magazine would be giving a CD away for free. I'd never seen such a thing before.

I heard a voice inside my own mind that said, "Buy that magazine. You need that CD!"

As all intuition teachers do, I ignored my intuition and scolded myself for being ridiculous. I walked briskly out of the concession shop and toward my gate. Way down the hallway and on up the escalator, I heard the voice again, this time nagging me with urgency: "GO BACK! Go back and buy that magazine! You need to hear what's on the CD!"

Finally coming to my psychic senses, I ran through the airport like a loon, dodging people at breakneck speed, and almost missed my plane. I found the little snack shop again and snatched the magazine off the rack, bought it and ran all the way to my gate. I tucked it in my carry on without looking at it and flew to the Isle of Man.

The next day, still feeling depressed, I went into the conference room where I teach. The big empty room is a sad affair before and after the students arrive. Utterly alone in the silent room, still sinking in the stillness of my own pain, I dropped the "Party Starter" into the CD player. I was more than a little perturbed that my spirit guides had made such a fuss over this cheesy looking CD that they actually made me double back in the Glasgow airport and almost miss my flight. What on earth could be so important that I need to go to all that trouble? I hit 'play.' The first song started:

> "Everybody's dancin' in the moonlight.
> Everybody here is outa sight.
> They don't bark and they don't bite.
> What a supernatural delight.
> Everybody's dancin' in the moonlight.
> Dancin' in the moonlight..."

But the magic has yet to end. Only last month, I was in bed recovering from a very painful surgery. The pain medication sent me down into the doldrums and I found myself surprisingly depressed. I had been contracted to write another book, a book about animals who save lives, a more clinical book than this one that would need dump-trucks full of tedious research. It would have no reference to magic, heaven, or Mr. Jones. Perhaps this attributed more to my depression than I was able to realize at the time.

One of my most beloved students, Yvette Knight on the Isle of Man sent me a care package of all my favorite British comforts: Cadbury dark hot cocoa mix, Columbian coffee from Tescos, and even a pair of cushiony house shoes. But with this box of goodies also came a big stuffed toy. It was a grey and white stuffed cat that was so dusty, it made me sneeze, and the glass eyes were just creepy enough for me to set it by my front door and await the next trip to Goodwill.

It was obviously a well-loved relic and may have spent many years in the back of Yvette's closet. But late one miserable sleepless night, I dragged myself into the living room, and snatched up that stinky old stuffed cat. In some obscure way, it reminded me of Mr. Jones. I took it to bed with me and slept with it in my arms.

The unthinkable happened. I'm not going to tell you, because I know you know. We're not in a world where we're allowed to believe that spirits can visit us through the bodies of stuffed animals, so I'm not going to say that out loud. I'll only say this. I had my first restful night's sleep in months, and although I woke up with a nose full of British dust mites, I also had Mr. Jones sleeping blissfully on my chest. He gave me a pointed lecture about how I simply must write this book about animal soulmates, despite the contract to write the other more commercial venture. He adamantly insisted that there are so many people out there who need this confirmation that the spirits of their animals live on and that's it's totally okay to love animals as much as we love people. ("So you fell in love with a house cat! So what? It was the best I could do at the time! It's nothing to be ashamed of. These things happen.) After he chewed me out, he told me he would channel the book himself and beam the information down from heaven.

So, I started to try to write this story, but every time I sat at my desk, I couldn't even see my computer screen through all the tears, so I'd give up. One day he must have been really frustrated with me because I heard him say: "Don't worry about how it will get written. Just start the project and I'll do the rest! But I need to change the name of my chapter! It should be called *Dancin' In The Moonlight!*"

One might think I had hallucinated the conversation so later the same day, I had a heated talk with the photo of Mr. Jones that adorns my bedside table.

"How do I know you're real?" I demanded. "And I don't want to write your nutty book! Do you really want me to write another crazy obscure book about some kooky phenomenon that no one will understand? I'm going to write something more commercial this time, not a book about conversations with dead cats! Who would ever understand something like that?!"

I was tearful and furious, so I didn't get a response. Meanwhile, my best girlfriends in Los Angeles had loaned me dozens of movies that I could watch in bed while I spent the two months recuperating from the operation. I had started watching a television series the day before that was loaned to me by my dear friend and student, a radiant pixie of a movie-star named Amy Smart. The show also starred Amy and depicted a family living through the turbulent 1970's in America. A half a dozen distractions kept me from finishing the show I had started, but suddenly, I had an instinctive urge to pop in the DVD. The telepathic nudge seemed to come from the vicinity of the photo of Mr. Jones framed on my bedside table, and the desire turned into an uncontrollable urge. Finally, I said, "Alright! Alright! What is it this time?"

"Finish the show!" he said. I unplugged the phone, socked in the DVD and crawled into bed. Within moments, I was engrossed in the show, just where I'd left off, but in this new scene my dear gorgeous girlfriend, Amy, was arguing with her on-screen boyfriend, a record producer. The record producer was in the studio with a newly discovered band, frustrated that he just couldn't quite make their new song work. The band was crooning, *"Singing in the moonlight. Everybody here is outa sight. They don't bark and they don't bite. What a supernatural delight. Everybody's singing in the moonlight."*

And then out of the mouth of one of my real life best friends came the words, "No! I don't want to *sing* in the moonlight! I want to *dance* in the moonlight! Change it to *dancing* in the moonlight!" The record producer swept her off her feet for a dizzying kiss and told her she was a genius. He made the correction, and thus the song was born.

The band immediately changed the words and the song began to sizzle. The song was like a celebration of passion once they finally found the right words: *"Dancin' in the moonlight..."*

I surrendered in that moment. This book is a tribute to all of you out there who have had a "Mr. Jones." My Mr. Jones and I will be dancing in the moonlight throughout eternity. Join our party and together we'll dance...some of us on two legs and some of us on four. Kick up your feet, and don't worry if your partner in this cosmic dance has paws, hooves, or wings. It's nothing to be ashamed of. These things happen.

2 LAUREN: SOME THINGS ARE FOREVER
By Kay Pfaltz

"I found in one small dog the love I'd been searching for throughout my life."

Every once in a while someone walks into our lives who will change it forever. Rarely do we see this at the start, sometimes not even in the midst, only realizing the full strength of love once it's left us. For when love comes to us, death as we know it, is put at bay—love, not life, being death's opposite or antidote—and when we find love, we also find death no longer a dreaded specter, but only a stage in eternal life. Death comes to all, taking from us physical lives we once loved and shepherding grief in life's wake, yet also offering us the chance to understand that everything we love lives on. I found this out the hard way. The greatest gift I ever received was a strange little dog. Her name was Lauren.

The first time I ever heard of Lauren I was in my apartment in Paris and my boyfriend of the minute had just broken up with me, for what seemed the eighty-eighth time. My sister Amy had been telling me to get a dog, get a dog. She said it would ease the loneliness, and I'd have something to care for, something to love, and something to force me out of the apartment. It would be a constant companion she said. Amy got a dog whenever she got depressed. That was her answer to life's curve balls. She had eleven dogs.

The phone rang and thinking it my boyfriend, or ex-boyfriend rather, I raced for it. It was Amy.

"You should get a dog," she said as I lifted the receiver. She must have had some extra sense to have known how bad things were.

"I don't want a dog. I want someone to talk to over candlelight dinners, someone to go to the movies with, someone—"

"Little Autumn and I talk," she interrupted.

"Interesting conversation, I want stimulating conversation, ideas—"

"Autumn and I have stimulating conversations all the time."

"That's you talking with yourself. You're starting to get eccentric, Amy. I just don't think a dog is what I'm looking for or the answer to my current problems. No offense to your coping mechanisms," I added.

"You never listen to me in the times you most need it. One day you'll see. Remember hindsight has…"

"…twenty-twenty vision," I finished for her.

"Well, learn from it. Don't keep making the same mistakes."

"You mean learn from you."

"Of course."

We hung up, but she phoned me back the following evening, excited.

"I have the dog for you! Her name's Lauren and she's adorable."

"Who's Lauren?"

"She's a little beagle, and you're gonna love her."

"Hold on a minute."

Beagles were a dime a dozen in Virginia where I had grown up and where Amy still lived. They were used as hunting dogs, and sometimes badly treated. Many were strays or came from beagle colonies where the dogs were used to test new products, some never seeing the outside light. Beagles were used in the laboratories because they were small, friendly and even-tempered. Mostly they were tortured in the testing, injections shot into them, minuscule cages, no windows.

"She a colony escapee?"

"Probably!" Amy liked that.

"Really, where'd you find her?" I asked.

"She found me. Well Autumn found her, really." Little Autumn was my sister's little terrier who I called, much to Amy's horror, a little bag of rags. "I was late for work but Autumn kept barking at something under the porch, so I went to investigate. That's when I saw her. She was unconscious, nothing but bones, covered in fleas. I checked her gums, white as they could be, so I knew I had to move quickly. If I'd have found her thirty minutes later, she would have been dead."

I didn't realize then, as Amy spoke, the magnitude of this single statement. I didn't realize my destiny was being shaped. I only asked, "Where's Lauren now?" curiosity overtaking sense.

"She's in intensive care. They wouldn't touch her until I raced back and got Apache to do a blood transfusion." Apache was Amy's German shepherd and I always told Amy the shepherd blood inside Lauren was the reason she would, time and again, develop crushes on big, male German shepherds. "Kay," my sister continued. "They wouldn't even give her a bath for fear she'd die right there in the tub. I mean, picture a tiny, flesh and bones dog, almost dead. I drove so fast to get home—I thought she'd be gone when I returned."

And years later when I'd get Amy to tell me the story over and over, I'd involuntarily hold my breath, as if willing Lauren to live and become a part of my life. "She has some disease," Amy continued, "like AIDS, where her blood cells keep attacking her immune system." She paused. "The vets said she's probably not going to make it, but I thought she ought to have a home to go to, just in case."

"I don't need a dog."

"Actually you do. You need Lauren."

That's how it all began. Lauren stayed in intensive care for three weeks. It was touch and go every day. Would her hermatocrits be up or down? Would she make it or not? The husband and wife vet team fell in love with her, as would many in her years to come. They absorbed some of the costs and alleviating Amy of what would have been enormous fees she could not have paid. But I had not thought much about Lauren after the phone conversation except to ask Amy once in a while when she called how the little beagle was doing.

As Lauren began to recover, my sister pressed me harder to take her.

"You'll love her."

But I didn't want a dog. Then she sent me the photograph. I still have that photo. We call it the orange one, because Lauren sits on a scrap of orange cloth out in Amy's back yard. It was love at first sight. Never had I seen a more vulnerable looking animal. She was skinny and pathetic, yet the expression on her face and in her big eyes was one of acceptance. Acceptance is different from resignation. Lauren had suffered and she, like most animals, had accepted it. I wanted to pull her close to my breast, stroke her, and never let her go.

I noticed a shaved spot on her front leg where the I V had been. How could I have known then the significance of that mark? That she would, over the years to come, rarely be without that shaved rectangular on her front leg, or, as time went on, on three of the four white legs. I phoned Amy when I got the picture.

"I want her." I was serious. Now I was afraid that Amy would give her to someone else, for she'd been asking all her friends when I'd been reluctant. Amy was excited, and felt vindicated.

"Lauren," I whispered. The little dog in the picture was three colors: black, brown and white on the underside. It was perched on tentative white legs and so thin I could count each vertebrae in the backbone. It had a crooked tail, with a white tipped end, big brown eyes the color of liquid tea that appeared to be lined with an eye pencil, and a beautiful brown face and head. But it was the look in the eyes that moved me the most. It looked lost.

This was the beginning of a love story. And yet I would not end up with Lauren for more than a year. One day my boyfriend, for whom I also worked, informed me that actually he was married and I'd have to resign. Grief turned to anger and then despair at the thought of losing both the job I loved and my boyfriend. I flew back to the states like a dog slinking into a cave, tail between legs. Little did I know I was to gain far more than I lost.

When I returned to Paris a little dog flew with me. I loved her on first sight and evidently she loved me, for Amy said she howled whenever I left. I would drive to Amy's house and spend hours stroking Lauren—she had the softest ears I'd ever felt—and gazing into her rich brown eyes until Amy caught me and made fun of us.

Not only did I return to Paris with Lauren but also with a new job. One evening in Virginia Amy and I had visited our dear friend, Linda, taking Lauren and Apache with us. Linda's father edited a monthly review of Paris whose actual name was something like Our Paris, but which he insisted on calling The Poop on Paris, and, in time, I further altered it to Paris Poop—appropriate I thought given the condition of some of the sidewalks in Paris. I was to be the restaurant, movie and concert reviewer.

Lauren was in good enough health to travel, and had gained weight so that now she was over the weight limit of seven kilos required if taking the dog into the cabin. But I ignored this fact for never would I place her or any dog in cargo. The conditions were erratic; the temperature could be either excessively hot or cold; the noise was loud; the animal would be all alone.

"And what if the plane crashes?" I howled at Amy. "I want to be with her."

"If the plane crashes you're dead and she's dead so it

really doesn't matter, does it?"

My obsession with plane crashes began with that first flight with Lauren. I'd flown all over the world and never cared a lick. But now I had something to care about.

I bought a little baby carrier that I could put Lauren in and strap to myself. I'd seen kids being carried in these before. This was in case the plane crashed into water and we were asked to jump into life boats. I didn't want anyone telling me, "People first. No dogs." She would be attached to me. She would come with me or I would refuse to jump.

I was amazed on that first flight over to Paris. She had never done this before in her life, and yet she behaved like a veteran flyer.

"Elle est très sage." The words I was to hear over and over. The word sage in French means far more than merely our "wise." It translates to well-behaved, virtuous, sensible, prudent, wise, good and, most of all, gentle. Lauren came to exemplify the full meaning of the word sage.

"Oui, elle est sage," I'd repeat.

People walked by and touched her. A German woman, observing her for a long time, declared, "She is so kind to everyone."

The plane touched down at Charles de Gaulle airport at 7:10 Paris time. I was glad that Lauren would soon be able to get out and walk around. When I felt the wheels jolt heavily, once or twice, on asphalt, I experienced that quick sudden thrill and familiar feeling. Only this time it was different. This time I felt different.

I grabbed a trolley, put Lauren's bag on top near my hands and opened it. Her head came out and she looked bleary-eyed, but again she stayed quiet, remaining in the bag with no struggling, merely observing the passengers pushing carts, as if she understood the process. Perhaps she did—or perhaps she knew I did, felt my calm and reacted to that. As I wheeled her along towards the luggage belt, I felt the looks and glances. Kids rushed up to stroke her.

"Mama, régard!"

"Oui, c'est un beau chien, cherie."

I knew Lauren would be good before I went, though there was every reason why she should not have behaved well, but I believed in her. She trusted me. And from that grew the strength of my relationship with this odd little dog. I respected her and, while I frequently laughed at her, I never did anything that would insult or damage her dignity.

The taxi zipped along past the ugly suburbs of Paris, and as we entered Paris' city limits, my heart beat faster. Lauren was partially in her bag and sound asleep. I nudged her.

"Look Lauren, there's Notre Dame." I said it quietly. The sun coming up over the buildings in the east touched the apse of the great gothic cathedral.

I'd seen Notre Dame de Paris from this view a hundred or more times and it still gave me chills. I looked at my arm: goosebumps, sure enough. I looked at Lauren: snores, sure enough. She was asleep again. Paris, big deal. We drove past the Jardin des Plantes, then up the rue Lacépède, stopping on the Place de la Contrescarpe before my apartment.

"Okay Lauren, let's go." I snapped the leash on her and let her jump out of the taxi, her paws touching the cobblestones of the Paris streets for the first time. She did a big stretch right in the middle of the road, as two mopeds swerved to avoid her. I jumped to her rescue, and paid the driver, who charged for every bag carried and of course for le chien. I let Lauren go to the bathroom then carried the bags up the short flight of steps to the apartment. It always smelled the same, a little musty. Lauren was sniffing around exploring her new lodgings. I inhaled deeply then opened the windows wide.

How the sounds of the outside and of the streets came to life with the opening of a window. From the café directly below, the talk, the laughter, the clink of glasses rose up to greet me. I shivered. Sun-warmed air filtered in and I stood gazing out. I saw no clochards, just couples strolling and holding hands, and looking at them this time I wasn't upset. The sun slipped in and out from behind puffy cumulus clouds and I turned and saw Lauren curled up sleeping on my sofa, the air from the open window gently blowing her ruff.

"Lauren, let's go!"

She hopped down and stood waiting before the door to her new home. I clipped on the long extension leash, and we walked out into the dark hallway, down the steps and out into welcoming bright sunlight.

My life with Lauren in Paris had begun. I knew where we were going, where I always went first. I wanted to show Lauren the Luxembourg Gardens. She trotted up ahead, at the end of the long leash, stopping frequently to sniff where male dogs had left their mark. She behaved as if she'd walked the history laden streets of Paris many times in her life. She didn't look up at the grandeur of the Pantheon when we passed it. She just trotted along, nose to the ground.

We walked along, me stopping and waiting for Lauren as she met other dogs, sniffing them directly, while I smiled at the owners. We passed children running and lovers holding hands, students reading and absorbing rays of sunshine. I looked over at the palace built for Marie de' Medici in the seventeenth century. I looked over to the unequal towers of St-Sulpice behind it. I looked all around me and saw the French living their individual lives. I was here; I was in Paris. I was standing in this place that I loved, this garden that I cherished, and I was not alone. I looked down and Lauren's brown eyes stared back up at me as if to say, "What are we stopping for?"

"Okay let's go." Lack of sleep was beginning to catch up with me, but I continued, wanting to share with Lauren all the places I loved. My boyfriend was still on my mind, but he'd become a log floating down a distant river. He would probably always be floating, but he would float farther and farther away from me.

All of a sudden the sharp, loud sound of a whistle broke my thoughts. Turning toward the piercing sound, I saw a guard walking pointedly toward me and waving his stick at Lauren.

"Mademoiselle! Pas de chiens! C'est interdit. Mademoiselle! No dogs! It's forbidden!"

"Ah bon? C'est interdit? Oh really? It's forbidden?" While in the years to come as this event happened over and over I would feign ignorance and put on my most atrocious American accent, which wasn't at all hard to do, this time I really was oblivious to the rule.

"Oui Mademoiselle. La bas seulement. Yes, Mademoiselle. Over there, only." And he directed me to the part of the park from where we had just come, the only part to allow dogs.

"Excusez nous. Excuse us." I retreated, pulling the illegal beagle along. So we strolled back the way we'd had come, but in future attempts Lauren and I would walk in the forbidden areas, my eyes always alert for the gendarmes. It elicited the same thrill as doing something forbidden as a kid. When I would hear the familiar shrill piercing blow of the whistle I would walk as though I were preoccupied, and I swear Lauren likewise would adopt a very guileless air about her.

On the way back to the apartment, Lauren decided to stride up to every restaurant, all now open and serving lunch, and proceed in through the door. Her long leash allowed it as I watched from the sidewalk outside. Diners smiled in amusement and the waiters, complicit to her prank, called her forth.

"Come on, Lauren. Let's go home." She turned her head and gazed forlornly back at me as if to say, "You never feed me." Did I ever feel guilty. She pulled this trick frequently and won the hearts of everyone around her, while I received wicked glares.

I did always feed her. It was called the Feeding Frenzy and the happiest time of day for her. She gulped down her food without, I believe, really tasting it, faster than any dog I'd ever seen—a small vacuum that ran without batteries.

That evening I did the Feeding Frenzy for the first time in Paris. It didn't really matter to Lauren, though—just as long as she got fed. I disguised her medication in bits of dog food.

I cooked fried eggs and French green beans for myself and went to bed early. Lauren slept next to me, her head on one pillow, mine on the other.

I quickly fell into a routine of writing my reviews in the morning about the film I'd watched the night before. Usually I went to the movies on the left bank for, from my apartment, I could walk there in fifteen minutes, ten if I hurried. I left Lauren alone in the apartment, and worried about her constantly throughout the movie, so much so that it greatly affected my feeling for the film. I'm not sure what I was afraid of; after all it was only for a matter of hours. But I guess my dramatic side took over and I started worrying about bombs going off in the cinema as it was a time of terrorism and many bombs. I can still hear Amy's gleeful laugh when I told her my latest train of thought and that I was counting on her to again rescue Lauren should I die, this time not from a plane crash, but from a bomb blast.

I decided to carry on me always in my wallet or in my carte orange a slip of paper that read on the outside: "En urgence," or Emergency. Inside would read, "In case of death, I have a little dog all alone in my apartment. She takes medication. Please call 1-804-295-1722," Amy's number, "and say that Lauren is all alone in the apartment." I made the mistake of showing this paper to my sister once and she laughed so hard I really did think she was going to have a stroke. Folded up with the note I also enclosed a fifty franc note, so whoever retrieved the paper would have enough money to call the United States. I still have that paper. I still have the fifty francs that went with it, even though, replaced by the Euro, the franc is now sadly obsolete.

I left the cinema in an agitated state, was assaulted by throngs of people waiting to see the next showing, and ran all the way home. I flung open the apartment door and there she was lying supine, white chest and tummy exposed, tail thumping in happiness, ears turned inside out in submission. I rubbed her stomach and kissed her as if I hadn't seen her in weeks. How many times had I returned to this apartment only to find it empty and myself still alone?

Not until I raised my head from her, though, did I notice for the first time Lauren's new arrangement of my apartment: The chair at my desk knocked over. The papers and books on the desk scattered all over the floor. The garbage can in the kitchen turned over, with debris strewn over the kitchen floor and out into the living room. I turned and looked at Lauren.

"What happened?" Her ears turned even more inside out. She groveled at my feet then flipped over on her back again. I never scolded her, just cleaned up the mess and tried to ignore her. That didn't last long.

When I told Amy about it, she explained that dogs get upset when we leave them. I understand only now that my worrying about Lauren during the movie communicated itself telepathically to her.

Lauren was no needy, neurotic dog (aside from a small vacuum cleaner phobia, but I learned this was not uncommon in dogs or, I should add, in some humans.) However, I could read panic in her eyes if I left her alone in strange places. If I had to run into a grocery store, I'd tie her outside and she'd stare at the doorway, the place she'd last seen me. When she'd first glimpse me coming back, her ears would lie back and she'd either roll over in obeisance or she'd bounce up and down like she did before being fed.

Thus my decision to take Lauren to the movies with me was a direct result of both our separation anxieties. We walked together over the familiar streets to Odéon, but a block away, I stopped, unzipped the bag and, in the middle of the sidewalk, gathered her into my arms and slipped her in. I put the bag once more over my shoulder, in an effortless way so no one would suspect live cargo, although it was now heavy with dog. Once in the movie house, I waited till the lights dimmed to unzip the bag and let her out. I didn't know how this would go, but her behavior was exemplary. She slept on my lap for part of the film and then hopped off and stretched out in the aisle. I heard the jingling of her tags at one point during the movie and looked over to see her twisting about on her back, in the middle of the carpeted walkway. She stopped and lay upside down, legs all spread out until a young man with a drink in each hand nearly tripped over her, walking down to his seat. But it didn't daunt her, for she just flopped over on her side and slept till the film finished.

We became quite adept at sneaking into the movies and I certainly think she preferred being there with me to being alone. These jaunts to the movies, however, were not trouble free. During a film, staring Isabelle Adjani, that I particularly wanted to see, Lauren would not behave. She refused to sit still and her rattling dog tags were beginning to disturb the audience. Heads turned around, as they will, to stare at me and nonverbally say, "Do something about it!" I didn't blame them, so I scooped her up and held her snugly on my lap.

It was only after the film ended, when the lights came back on, and the people luckily had forgotten about the earlier commotion, that I noticed the source of Lauren's agitation. There under the seat before me were two or three kernels of popcorn.

Shortly after I'd begun work for my new job as a reviewer, I got a phone call.

"Hello?"

"I'm coming over." It was my brother, Ted. He'd been discussing the possibility of taking some time off to spend with me in Paris, and now it was definite.

Ted arrived on a beautiful crisp October morning. Lauren and I met him at Charles de Gaulle and we all three jumped in a taxi for Paris. He loved food as Lauren and I did and together we would pour through the guidebooks selecting the perfect bistro to try out.

It was on a purely Parisian afternoon, when excitement hangs in the air like a great bird about to land, and everybody is out walking towards a rendez-vous, that Ted and I strolled along the boulevard du Montparnasse. The evenings were growing dark earlier, but it was around three in the afternoon so plenty of light still remained. Long shadows cast themselves along the streets as the sun moved west across Paris. People hustled by with bouquets of flowers or baguettes in hand.

I was hungry as we hadn't eaten since breakfast, and suddenly I turned to Ted and said, "Let's get lunch!"

"We can't eat out."

"I feel like eating out. Besides you've never been to the Coupole. It's a Parisian landmark. Each of the columns inside is painted by a different artist. Come on."

"But we can't," he protested.

"Why not?"

"The weasel!" he pointed to the pavement where Lauren, whom he had nicknamed "the weasel," stood in oblivious innocence.

"Kay, that dog is fanatical about food. I've never seen anything like it before and I'm sure I never will again. She'll be all over the table and lunging for everyone's plate. Be reasonable, and don't embarrass us both."

"She'll be fine. I know she will. Come on." Ted, ever cool, was noticeably upset. I knew he was reluctant to follow me, but I guess his desire for food overcame him.

Even though I had seen dogs in restaurants before, I waited for the maitre d' to tell me my dog had to go. No one said a word and Lauren trailed along beside me on her leash, alert to the robust aromas of food. The great brasserie was still crowded and bustling from the lunch crowd, but thinning out a bit as people returned to work. We walked by soiled linen tablecloths, with half glasses of wine and water left standing, past gray heads bent forward in animated conversation, until we arrived at our table and I slipped in on the red banquet and put Lauren right beside me. Ted sat across from us.

"Hold her tight," he whispered.

"Don't worry." I had my arm around and in front of her so she couldn't climb on the table. The waiter took our order and then turned and asked if Lauren might like some water. Yes, thank you very much, she might. He came back with a bottle of Sancerre on ice and a chilled Badoit for us and placed before Lauren a sterling silver water bowl. Such was Lauren's introduction to French dining, and I knew from that moment that I'd done the right thing.

Lauren was so well-behaved, I was proud, but also I was thrilled because it meant I could take her with me from now on, with or without company, whenever I ate out. Apart from outdoor cafés, La Coupole was her first restaurant, and it would be here that we'd return to celebrate her birthday each year. Since we never really knew her real birthday, I asked Amy to look on her calendar and tell me the date she discovered Lauren. She did. It was August the 8th. All my friends looked forward to Lauren's birthday celebration at the Coupole as if it were the big event of the year. I marveled at her devoted following.

By the time we left La Coupole it was growing dark outside. The lights were coming on in apartment buildings and the yellow headlights crowded the great boulevards. The briny taste of seafood lingered in our mouths as the wine tingled in our bodies.

"October already, and I don't know where September went. Is that part of the human condition, our bizarre obsession with time? We're continually losing it, and I know few people who've ever found it again."

"She doesn't lose it," Ted nodded at Lauren. And I knew he was right. I knew that on some level, conscious or not, she accepted time, or its lack, in its truest essence, the present moment. What's the meaning of life? Go ask your dog.

It was with and because of Lauren that I learned much about myself, and about others as well. Evidently all the things other people discovered years ago. I'm essentially a loner, but like every other human being from time immemorial, I needed other people—and, I wanted love. I thought I was easy-going and giving. I thought I was passionate and romantic. I worked well when coupled and I would've lived my whole life that way, had the choice always been left up to me. Why then, while in that wonderful couple, did my most meaningful moments happen alone? Lauren helped me solve this conundrum, for I was able to share fully with her what I couldn't always share with a lover. I realized that even in love, our most significant events are ultimately individual experiences.

"Twit-brain, it's because you can be yourself with her." Amy was less than tolerant of my revelations so late in life. "You don't lose your independence. That's what we humans are all searching for—to retain our separate selves, yet have a union with another. It's the human condition to want the impossible. If we got it—being human, an only moderately intelligent life form—we'd no longer long for it. We want to be accepted for who we are no matter what, and loved unconditionally. And who does this for us?" Pause. "Twit-brain, I'm talking to you."

"Yeah."

"Who does this for us? Our animals, that's who."

I could not ignore how fate insisted that I love this dog. We were two souls destined to be together. Two like-souls. She was to the canine race what I was to the human race. I can explain it no better than that. She was different. I was different. Together, we were alike. She stood beside me in all situations, and yet I knew she would not complete this life with me as a human mate might have. Yet, when I thought about it, it was Lauren who was my companion in life. I found in one small dog the love I'd been searching for throughout my life.

Lauren spoke to my soul. When I looked at her I saw everything in life I loved. She was honor, truth, courage, beauty and love. I have never pretended to understand love. It is either life's greatest gift or a human attempt to create something divine. I realized Lauren had taught me more than any creature on earth, for she'd taught me about love. Maybe that's why we're put on this earth, to learn how to love. When E.M. Forster wrote, "Only connect," I don't think he was referring to a stray beagle, but then we each do the best we can.

Lauren and I were inseparable. Together we walked every cobblestone of Paris. From Montmartre to the Butte aux Cailles, the Butte Chaumont to the parc Montsouris. The gardens of the Palais Royal, the Champs de Mars, and Lauren's favorite, the rose garden in the Bagatelle. No longer alone in Paris, I was filled with something beyond joy…a sense of peace. We dined side by side like an old couple, in comfortable silence, Lauren always upright beside me in her own chair, or sometimes on the banquet next to me. She had become so much a part of me I could not imagine life with out her.

But then came a day different from all the rest. Lauren had been plagued throughout her life with various illnesses, but in the ninth year of her life, after I had returned to Virginia to be closer to her U.S. vets, she was diagnosed with transitional cell carcinoma, a fancy name for a very aggressive cancer that had formed a tumor at the base of her bladder, blocking her urethra and making urination impossible. I didn't want to euthanize her just because she couldn't go to the bathroom. On the other hand, I didn't want her to suffer from invasive treatments. To a person you can say, "Okay, you're going to feel awful for a while, but it's for your own good." Could I make Lauren understand this? The only hope I had to reduce the size of her tumor was radiation therapy at the Veterinary Referral Center. I decided I would go ahead and try.

The Veterinary Referral Center boarded dogs undergoing radiation therapy, but at this point in our lives, I couldn't have left Lauren there alone. Where I went, she went. And where she went, I went.

Dr. St. Vincent met us the first day and examined Lauren. I listed all of Lauren's medications and explained all her various conditions. Then the doctor explained to me the procedure. Lauren would have radiation therapy every day for twenty sessions. For this she would have to be put under anesthesia for about fifteen or twenty minutes. In conjunction with this, she also recommended chemotherapy once a week. Would Lauren lose her appetite for food? Would Lauren feel miserable? I'd heard horror stories from people who'd been subjected to chemotherapy. But it was the anesthesia that scared me the most.

"Isn't it a risk with her laryngeal paralysis?" I asked, trying to sound normal.

"Well yes, we'll give her a shot, ten minutes before that will help her heart rate."

"Could I come be with her?"

"No. We can't let you in the radiation room."

"If something were to happen, would you... come get me, so I could be with...."

"We've never lost a dog under anesthesia."

"Do you have a high success rate with this?"

"If all goes well, she could have six months, maybe up to a year."

I didn't at first speak. When I did it came out funny. "Up - to - a - year?"

"Yes. The diagnosis is always guarded with cancer of the bladder or urethra. It's a very difficult cancer to treat effectively."

I found I had nothing to say. Why was I putting Lauren through all this, if she only had "up to a year?" But now it was too late to turn back. Dr. St. Vincent led me into a waiting room with a soft sofa and chair, and within minutes a vet tech, named Kate, gave Lauren her premeds. Then Bob, another technician carried her away, and I wondered if I'd ever again see Lauren alive.

Exhausted, for in the past three or four days I'd slept very little, I lay my head back against the sofa in the small waiting room. I watched dogs come and go, listened to voices and wondered what was happening to my dog. Life and death intermingled. I floated in and out of conscious thought. I discovered that each individual moment was benign, free from disease. Each moment, isolated from memories of the past or fear of the future was joy; no clouds, no shadows. Lauren. Don't think.

After twenty minutes, I anticipated seeing her again. After thirty minutes I started looking around for one of the vet techs. After forty-five minutes, I stood and walked to the front desk. The receptionists were all busy talking to people.

Then an hour had passed. Then an hour and a half... an hour and forty-five minutes....

I sat back against the sofa wondering if Lauren were dying now and if I should bust into the radiation room to say goodbye. She'd probably die because she thought I'd abandoned her, like her first owners. Maybe if she saw me, she'd fight to live. She probably thought I'd left her alone to die because she'd been so much trouble. Why can we not be with our loved ones when they need it most, to give a reassuring nod, a squeeze of the hand...or paw?

In that instant I knew Lauren had died under anesthesia and they were afraid to come tell me. In that instant I knew I would give up everything I owned to be able to raise my head and see them bringing her back to me. I would gladly give up the things I value most: the sun as it touches my face in the morning, the air as it blows the Virginia pines. Just to watch her one more time twist and squirm on her back.

"Here she is. She was perfect, but she's still waking up from the anesthesia, so why don't you two wait here for a bit," Kate said and Bob set Lauren gently on the sofa beside me. She looked groggy and dazed as though she was just recovering from a hard night out. But she was here.

"Lauren," I whispered.

"She was under longer than usual. The first session always takes the longest. Dr. St. Vincent had to map her out."

"Map...?"

"For the radiation. See? She's shaved here, and marked. Don't wash this off."

I looked at Lauren's hip where she'd been shaved in a funny pattern, an X and some lines, a rectangular spot, but the oddest part were the marks made in black and green ink. She had dashes and dots and lines as if tattooed onto her shaved skin. She looked like a punk rock dog that belonged to the underground stations of London, not to the conservative world of Northern Virginia.

"We'll come back and give her some salami sticks. Make sure she's swallowing. You were a good girl, sweetie." Smiling, Bob reached tenderly to stroke Lauren. Lauren turned her head and gazed up at me with bleary, brown eyes.

For a month Lauren and I lived at the Motel 6 in Springfield, Virginia, Monday through Friday. We'd go home on weekends. Lauren accepted her treatment with the understanding and perseverance that had distinguished her throughout all her traumas.

At first she still had to keep the catheter in, and I would empty it regularly with a syringe. After chemo treatments, I'd wear thick rubber gloves. But as the tumor gradually shrank, Lauren could go to the bathroom on her own. We'd accomplished what we'd set out to do.

I got used to arriving at the vets, sitting in the waiting room until Lauren was given her premeds then carried away to radiation. Some days were difficult with a poignancy that hurt for I realized most owners at the Veterinary Referral Center were treating their dogs so that the problems would be resolved—dogs, for instance, with melanomas on their legs and hips that, with radiation, would disappear. I seemed to be the only one who was there with a dog whose cancer was essentially incurable. Lauren looked better than many of the dogs, and yet within the year I could expect her to be gone.

I got used to living in the grungy little hotel, eating out of a cooler, because I couldn't afford to eat out. I got used to walking Lauren up and down the steps and out into the parking lot, with her strange punk dog markings, stares and questions coming from other residents of the hotel. Sometimes we drove to nearby Lake Accotink Park where we'd stroll for hours. Time slowed down. I thought her last day of treatment was something intangible, beyond our grasp, but then at last, it came.

And in the car driving home, I couldn't contain my joy. I

cried silently, all the while stroking Lauren beside me and stating, "We made it. We made it. You made it, Lauren."

She lay beside me on the seat wearing a white bandana with new age positive affirmations that the vets had given her after her last treatment. She also wore a little knotted up white T-shirt with a harness over it to keep her from biting the Fentenal patch on her side. The patch was to help her with pain.

Yes, we'd accomplished what we'd sought, but it was not without a price. While the chemotherapy did not seem to upset Lauren, the radiation did. The worst did not occur until after we'd been home. One day, as I was attempting to swab Silver Sulfadiazine cream onto her sores, she snapped her head around and simply stared up at me with pleading eyes. She was in pain and would have snapped at me, but could not bring herself to do it. I stared back at her and in her look I saw the toll physical suffering takes on a being. What I had sought so hard to avoid, I had caused.

The darkest moment that I have ever known came one evening, sitting on my bed beside Lauren. I had finally realized that I must use the Elizabethan collar. Wearing the collar, Lauren looked up at me with an expression of pure misery. Then she began to flop around like a fish out of water. I tried to comfort her, but she didn't want to be touched. So I sat there, impotent, unable to relive even some of her suffering, and I realized I had made an irrevocable error. I had failed the one being I loved most in the world.

But then, like the sun breaking through clouds after a steady rain, Lauren began to heal. Her good spirits came back, and then so too did mine. She regained her appetite. I fed her multiple vitamin supplements and changed her to a raw food diet, pureeing fresh vegetables for her weekly.

Slowly our old life came back to us, yet differently; the abiding specter of cancer, not forgotten, but not allowed center stage either. We had to get on with living.

And it was Lauren who taught me to enjoy these moments that would never come back to me. Perhaps the knowledge that her loss was now so inevitable made the having sweeter still. Many the moment when I would stop, and in some Faustian trance, look at her and speak silently to myself:

"Stay moment stay. Thou art so fair."

I knew that I loved this dog in a way that I had never felt before and realized I would never feel again. Maybe it's true what they say about everlasting love coming along once in a lifetime. Mine would have to be with a dog.

Lauren lived twenty-one months from the time she was diagnosed with cancer, twenty-one months that were not without anguish and pain, but months made up of days and weeks and hours that never once did I take without gratitude. Lauren was accepting, patient and trusting. She had good days and bad days, but on the bad days she never complained. She lived each day as it came, in the present, not worrying over the past or projecting to the future. And when I did things to her she didn't like, she chose forgiveness over revenge. The more I watched her the more I was humbled. I believe she taught me more than a shelf of self-help books.

When she developed a new tumor making urination again impossible, I knew I would put her to sleep. I had promised her that if the cancer returned I would not put her through any more procedures. It was a heartbreaking decision to make, one that would of course forever alter our lives, ending hers as I knew it, and in some ways ending mine too. But I had always made my decisions with what I believed was right for Lauren, not myself. I looked deep into my heart and knew what we both now had to do.

During her last week she lived with a catheter so she and I could spend these final days together at home, not at the vets. And while her body had begun to fail, her spirit never did. For weeks I had not left her side, often crying silently though trying not to so she wouldn't see. But of course she knew. Her last days were like none I had ever before known. I didn't want to see or be with anyone but her, because very soon I knew I would never see or be with her again. How strange, having decided to end a life, the days, the hours, the minutes just ticking by—my heart breaking with every tick, and fear looming larger as each day gave in to nightfall. But for the moment, she was still here. I'd tell her at every chance, "I love you, Lauren." And she'd throw her head back and gaze up at me.

She grew more and more tired. Lauren had a tremendous will to live and I think she would have gone on trying to live, even in great pain, for as long as she could, just to be near me. Her way of taking care of me, just as I had always taken care of her. I tried to stay happy and cheery for her sake, but when she cried and looked so dejected, I too cried and knew I was making the right decision for her. But there were also times when she looked and acted just like her old self and in these moments we carried on, her living as she always had, me feeling the profundity of life and living more in the present than I ever had before, entering her world, the animal way of life, because of her. And in those moments there was perfection.

One of the things we did that we both loved—one of the only things that worked to sooth me at my most sad—was to sit together on her chair. I'd rub her stomach or head or back and read to her from the galley of her book. She loved it, and always without fail, and almost immediately, felt right to sleep.

On her last morning I was at a loss. My fear was growing. Reading was the only thing I could think of to do. After we'd risen and she'd sniffed the outside air for the last time, I lifted her onto her chair and perched beside her, stroking her and began reading to her about our life together. She'd doze off, then look up at me as if to tell me something. I'd talk to her and she'd doze off again. I would read, cry, stroke her, talk to her, begin to read again. I was half way through Chapter 43 when I heard wheels on the gravel drive outside my house. It was my vet. I panicked. I didn't do or say anything, but my heart started pounding and a terrible, frightening fear filled me. But I kept on reading till I finished the chapter. Then I told her I loved her.

The days and weeks and months after were a dull but constant pain, and I was stunned to realize how much grief felt like fear. Nothing seemed right. I had lost my will to live. Perhaps on the surface I appeared little changed to those around me, but each night I prayed that I might be allowed to follow Lauren to wherever she'd gone.

What is it we remember in life? The important? The trivial? The horrifying?

I remembered the grayish-brown face of a dog, lying upside down on her back gazing at me, telling me she loved me with just her quiet brown eyes. I remembered the white face of a dog sleeping peacefully in one small patch of sunlight, crescent eyes shut tightly. I remembered what life was like with a small dog who became my soul mate.

But now she was gone. Being with Lauren had been like being home. It didn't matter if I were in Paris or Virginia, wherever she was was my home. Now, I was lost. Days turned to weeks. Her book was published one month after she died. I didn't want it, only her. I continued to pray to be with her, but, as the months passed, I started asking not that I die but that we be closely connected forever, in whatever form that took.

The first time I saw Lauren again after she died, she came to me in a dream. Where photos, videos and memory had not even begun to bring her back to me or produce anything like the flesh, blood, heart and soul of the dog I had known, the dream made up for the desolate, painful, and grief-stricken months that had followed her leaving. She came to me warm, and healthy and smiling, wagging her tail in greeting. I stroked her and stroked her all the while saying, "Loor-ren, Loor-ren," as I always had. When I woke I felt close to her in a way my own reminiscence and the hundreds of photos around the house could not duplicate. I awoke speaking softly to myself, "How is it possible to feel that? And feel it in a dream?" I wondered only then which was real, the dream, or the waking life? I knew my answer, but would keep it quiet from all but a few.

As time went on, she would come to me in my dreams. I would ask each night before sleep, "Lauren please come to me." Then as the months turned to years, so did Lauren change from coming to me as Lauren the beagle I had known, to other forms in the dreams. Yet it was always her. I always recognized her in the dream, always connecting with her, even if she was not in the form of the dog I'd once known.

Then one morning I understood: the connection I was making was to her soul. It was her soul that visited me in my unconscious sleep, and the reason why she could come not as a beagle at all and I would always recognize her. It was her soul I had, and still, loved. I'd wake feeling astonished, full of joy and love. Lauren was still teaching me about love—to see beyond appearances. I had loved her beagle body, her "canister" as a friend called it, and after she died, I wanted that back. The furry, soft body and wet nose and quiet brown eyes. But it was her spirit who kept returning to me, or in fact, had never left me.

The dreams were the first in which I was to meet her again, and I suspect this was because, during those first anguished months when I tried too hard to find evidence of her, I was stressed, depressed, and unhappy, the farthest thing from the relaxed peace of mind one usually needs to contact those on the other side. Only in my sleep, my mind unconscious, did I stand a chance at relaxing enough to allow her to break through that sorrowful energy that must have surrounded me in those sunken days.

The years passed and I came to know great joy in living with first one, then two, and now three wonderful dogs. As I became peaceful in the house and yard and hills where I had lived and walked with Lauren, so too did I begin to sense her more and more.

And now I still find her in the oddest places, in the oddest moments: a sudden sense of "knowing" as the breeze brushes my bare arms; a glimpse at the old linoleum on which she used to lie before I replaced it with stately tile. Beautifying and bettering my house was hard when it was upon the ugly old carpet or the tacky white linoleum that Lauren's small feet once walked.

The period following Lauren's death was one of great stress and crisis for me, but also one of accelerated growth. During one particularly hard spell, when I'd received difficult news, I walked outside and called to Lauren. I also asked for more light in my life. I went to work and went about my day as usual. That evening after turning out the lights, I sat down in Lauren's chair before going to bed. I closed my eyes and tried to call her to me. When I opened them, the house was still as it was, all dark, but my eye caught something on the rug below my feet. I called the rug "the tree-of-life rug" because its design was of a tree offering shelter to all kinds of animals. There by my left foot was a tiny gold star. I don't know from where it dropped, but I held it in my hand trying to understand the message I'd received. The tiny star had five perfect points. I kept staring, but no message came. Finally I went to bed. I woke at 4:30 to find my bedroom light was on. I had not turned it on, and there is no way for it to turn itself on. I returned to sleep leaving the light on, but as the dawn began to break I rose, as if beckoned by the light. I walked outside into the cold and when I looked up, I saw the star. One star. Just like the one I'd found the night before. It sparkled before me, and I saw five distinct points. Finally I had gotten the message. As day began, this one star, Sirius the dog star, was the only one bright enough to still be seen and it reigned in the sky together with the moon.

"Lauren!" I called, waving and smiling, but as morning sun brought more and more light, it became dim. I kept going out to check on the star which rose higher and higher, growing fainter and fainter, until, the last time, I could see it no more.

And yet. I knew that when my mortal eyes ceased to see this star, it would not be gone. It is always there. Just as Lauren, invisible to me, is still and always here.

Now I find many "signs." Are they Lauren? I think the messages are there for all of us, psychic or not-so-psychic. We just have to open our eyes, our ears and perhaps most of all our hearts. The most pervasive but also the most subtle is simply a sense of knowing that fills me with great calm. Knowing I can survive loss; knowing death is not the end, for all life is a continuum; knowing Lauren is always with me, and knowing that I loved.

And now, although her physical presence is gone from my life, nothing has ended. As I walk the streets of Paris, a little dog walks forever beside me.

Thank you, Lauren. Some things are forever.

(Kay Pfaltz is a writer and animal activist. Profits from her books are donated to animal welfare groups. Parts of this were excerpted from *Lauren's Story: An American Dog in Paris*.)

3 PEPPER: PLAYING POSSUM
by Susan Chernak McElroy

*"'Sometimes the best defense is no defense at all...' Suddenly, I think of
Pepper and grin. Is this a celestial choir kind of moment? Are the
clouds parting to reveal the face of God? No. This is just me smiling
with my hands in my cold pond, and my thoughts on a gentle, rickety
possum and on the gentle, rickety softness of my own crone body. I have
nothing to defend myself against in this moment."*

I thought she was a Siamese kitten, rolling around and
playing in the leaves behind my house. I thought, "Hmmm,
who has a new kitty?" But then, in the dappled forest light,
she morphed suddenly into her true self: Not a kitten but a
possum. Not just a possum, but a small, female possum with
eight babies in her pouch, each the size of a split pea.
     She was not just a young possum mother, but a possum
mother covered in maggots, unable to walk, emaciated, with a
prolapsed rectum. Not rolling in the leaves in play, but
dragging herself on her side to escape the flies crawling all
over her. I guess the possum gods were not done with me
this summer. My fostered baby possums were raised and
released by now, but now this pathetic creature had found her

way to my door. Evidently, there was more I needed to learn about possums.

In the house, I called out to my husband, "Carter! There's a hurt possum in the holler!" He called back, "There's a song in there somewhere…" He's used to my bringing up all sorts of creatures from the steep hollow at the back of our property. Some of them need help. Some of them, I just bring in to show him ("See this turtle! See this frog? See, this huge bug!?"). His response is always enthusiastic. I don't know if his delight is real, or faked for my sake, but God bless him in either case.

Before dashing back outside, I put in a call to WildCare, the small but valiant wildlife rehabilitation center I volunteer with in Bloomington, Indiana. Each wildling that finds it way into WildCare's sphere sets off a string of paperwork, which follows that animal til death or release. I ran into the garage for a towel, then raced back down the hill to chase away the flies and gather the possum up in my hands. She was light as a feather, nothing but a small mound of bones and matted fur. Her eyes had that glazed, "I'm-checking-out-of-here-really-soon" look to them. Several of her babies dropped away, dead. The possum was straining hard, pushing out her red bottom like an inverted melon. I did not know then that she was trying to force out the wad of parasites and worms in her tummy. At that moment, all I could see was her behind crawling with maggots.

Where to start when everything seems to be wrong? I gave her some fluids in a syringe, and eased her into my kitchen sink for a warm bath. In my hands I held an eyebrow comb and a toothbrush. Working as quickly as I could, I combed away the maggots, fly eggs, old scabs and old poop stains. I washed her gently with a mild shampoo, then toweled her off and sat down with her in my lap. This summer, I purchased a set of magnifying lenses you can wear on your head, like a jeweler. With them, I was able to find more maggots I'd missed, so tiny I could not see them with my glasses alone. I picked them away.

In the possum's pouch, her three remaining babies were also covered in small maggots, which had eaten their way into the babies' flesh. I pulled the tiny, embryonic infants away. They were far beyond help. Their mother looked far beyond help, too, but my hands kept working away, of their own mind it seemed.

I had planned to spend that day preparing for out of state company. Instead, I spent it on the phone, on the Internet, and on the floor where I work best. I put a tiny drop of hydrogen peroxide into each open wound around the possum's head and neck, flushing the bugs and eggs away. Along with all her other misfortunes, mama possum bore the marks of a recent scrap with a dog or some other biting creature.

Her skin felt like clay, indicating severe dehydration. I kept offering her fluids in small amounts and she didn't fight them. She had no fight left. But she had a heart---a big one, I would learn.

By evening, she had taken some food. I'd injected her with fluids to rehydrate her more quickly. The maggots and fly eggs were gone. She was resting quietly in a plastic tub on old fleece throws and an absorbent pad. I'd managed to get her anus back inside where it belonged.

That night, I talked to Greta, my possum team leader, about yet one more perplexing symptom I'd come across in the course of my maggot hunting. The possum was covered head to toe in hard, white bumps the size of the head of a pin. The bumps were under her skin, on and in her rectum, eyeballs, ears, lips, toes. She had hundreds of them, sort of like the bumps you see on a plucked chicken leg. Greta said she'd call the National Opossum Society, and see what she could find out, not just about the bumps, but about the proper medications for everything else we were dealing with.

When I finally turned off the lights that night for bed, I gave the possum a reassuring stroke on her bumpy head. She looked at me fixedly. She could not close her eyes. She could blink, but whatever those bumps were, they kept her from pulling the lids down over her eyes to sleep. I did not hold much hope that she would survive until morning. I decided to call her "Pepper," thinking it was a name that had some fire to it, and this little lost one would need all the fire she could muster to reignite her life.

Pepper was still alive the next morning! She seemed eager for some food. She had pooped in the night, and her feces were so full of worms of many kinds, the gooey pile could have walked away under its own power. Yech.

Company was coming in three hours, a friend and her son I hadn't seen in years. I threw on my clothes and drove off to WildCare for medications, starting her on different wormers and antibiotics than those I had at home for emergency care. Greta suggested some Geritol for Pepper's probable anemia. I brought home specially made frozen possum food, syringes, high-calorie food in a tube, and special care liquids to strengthen her.

My mind was in three places at once: With my husband, who had left the day before to visit his kids for a week, with my girlfriend who'd be arriving for a week's stay momentarily, and with Pepper. These days, my mind has a hard time being in even one place at a time. I felt fractured, foggy, and anxious.

Pepper watched me, yawned now and then, and gratefully gobbled up her medications like they were possum candy. She resisted nothing I did to her---not the injections, the butt probing, the fluids, or the quick rinse-offs when she messed herself.

I made her up a special lunch of possum food, yogurt, baby food, and grapes. She ate so loudly, her lips smacked. When she was finished, she made motions of pushing the food away. I finally realized she was making a valiant-hearted attempt to wash her face, which she could not quite manage. On the floor, she could go nowhere but creep in a tight circle. Pepper could not move her back end. Or much of her front end. Her head was too heavy to lift.

That evening, we got word from the National Opossum

Society that Pepper's many bumps and hardened skin were the result of a particular parasite inside of her. The possum expert emailed us, "You think the bumps look bad outside? Sorry to say she has many, many more inside, on her organs, her nerves, her intestines---everywhere." I was advised of some medication changes needed, and that if Pepper survived at all, it would be a long haul. The bumps would take weeks or more to resolve, and the die-off of the parasites, plus the liver-damaging medications, would take a hard toll on a weak, starved body. The parasites could also be the reason for her neurological problems. It would take a long time to tell.

My visiting friend, Debbie, came by for dinner with her son Max and they watched Pepper struggle her way through her evening meal. They took some photos of her. Then they looked at her hunched on her pink towel and said, "Wow, she looks really bad!" I wish I could have disagreed...

A few weeks passed, and Pepper didn't die. Her wounds healed slowly. She gained weight. The small white bumps began a slow retreat, and her hair began growing back over her bald back legs. As she moved forward through crossroads of healing, I came to a crossroads in my own life.

I decided to give away all my chickens and rabbits. Keeping caged and penned creatures was something I deeply sensed was over for me. I had become more and more sensitive to feelings of guilt and anxiety about having animals in situations that were far from optimal for them. I no longer have the stamina or the focus to provide a rich, diverse life for all the critters I needed to keep confined. So, off they all went to better circumstances. My sorrow in seeing them all go was mitigated by an overwhelming sense of relief that I would no longer have that nagging sense of inadequacy about their daily care and confinement.

Yes, I could have built roomy ground pens for the bunnies, and somehow constructed a much larger roaming pen for the chickens---who were becoming cranky and mean in smaller quarters. And yet, I couldn't. Money, energy, and ability were no longer at my fingertips for such an undertaking. Everything inside me said, "Let go. Don't expand and don't fret. The time for these tasks in your life is over. Just let go." And so I did.

You must be wondering what any of this has to do with Pepper Possum. Bear with me. It all comes around. Pepper Possum came to me more compromised than any wildling I had ever taken under my care. Any one of her problems was more than enough to deal with. In concert, they were overwhelming. My 'normal" life went away in caring for her. My new routine became phone calls and research and trips to the drugstore. My already fogged brain just sort of imploded, but somehow, my hands kept functioning, a day---an hour--- at a time.

"Give it three more weeks and we'll reassess her, if she survives that long," Patty, the Big Kahuna of Opossums, advised us.

Three weeks? How could any living thing survive such misery for that long?

Pepper survived her first full month with me. By the end of it, her rectum was healed, her pouch was drying up nicely, and she was eating well. The worms in her poop were showing up in slightly lesser numbers. But she could still only crawl around in a tight circle, her back legs dragging along behind her.

Each morning, I bypassed my meditations and early morning exercises to stumble downstairs and check on Pepper's status. Each morning, she remained alive but very still. I learned to make up her day's food the night before, and make sure her laundry was always fresh and clean. Our day would begin with me holding a dropper of cherry-flavored antibiotic to her nose. The heavenly scent would wake her up and she'd lick, lick, lick the medicine. Next came a dropper of Geritol. Lick, lick, lick. Then some worming medicine. Lick, lick, lick, lick. And finally breakfast, accompanied by much lip-smacking. I held her on my lap so she could put her long nose down in the food dish. She also liked to put her hands into the dish, and smear the food all over herself and me. She was weak and spastic, but she was enthusiastic, God bless her.

Next usually came a bath or some sort of cleanup. Then bedding changes, dishes, and perhaps some time on the floor for her so I could see if she was moving any better. She wasn't. Then came my bath and cleanup. We did this same routine several times a day, interspersed with more bedding changes, a dose or two of subcutaneous fluids, and lots of gentle pats and strokes and baby talk.

I told my husband I had not planned for this. I told him I was tired and uncertain about what came next. My hands kept up the work. Pepper hung on. I was told to keep her on her medication for at least three months. THREE MONTHS! And I knew in my bones I hadn't the stamina for such intense, critical care nursing. Three months?

One morning, Pepper pushed herself up clumsily in my lap and managed to slobber all over her pink hands and wash her face. It was a celebratory moment---I took them where I could get them. A couple days later, she actually managed to get her back legs beneath her and crawl jerkily across the carpet. When she flopped on her side, she managed to right herself with a great deal of effort, and crawl a couple more inches. I gave her a tablespoonful of strawberry yogurt for her efforts. Lick, lick, lick. Slobber, slobber. Big yawn. Pee.

In the midst of Month Two, Pepper's skin began sloughing off more of the white bumps. Her back because covered with orange, crusting skin. One eye continued to weep milky liquid. Between feedings and cuddles, she lay quietly. I read that the parasites cause a lot of discomfort and pain. She was still not able to shut her eyes, ever.

One night, her chest became congested and phlegmy. It came on instantly. The next morning, I hurried downstairs to see if she was still breathing. She was.

I was tired and muddle-headed, struggling daily to do what I cannot do well anymore. I reflected often on why Pepper came to me, and then reflected on why I even tried to reflect about this. I searched for meaning, and watched myself search. I tried to look ahead and imagine some kind of resolution for Pepper, and for myself. Best for Pepper would be if she could regain her ability to walk, and perhaps become an education animal. Best for me would be a clear diagnosis of chronic depression and a new course of medication that would actually work. I had no idea how much of the foggy, muddle headedness and deep fatigue of those days was related to age and how much of it might be deep depression. All I knew was that I found myself needing to make my life smaller and smaller. First, the chickens and the rabbits left. Then, I closed down my writing business. I took on less wildlife care. I stopped traveling and doing retreats and lectures. Pepper came along in the midst of the end of life as I had known it.

I considered having a pow-wow with the folks and WildCare to see if there was someone who could take on Pepper's journey for a longer term. But I didn't. Because Pepper was so dear to me. I was drawn deeply to her courage, her good humor, her unstoppable will to heal. She was my mentor as I wandered along my own foggy path of healing. For a brief break, my friend Beverly took Pepper in for a couple of weeks, and lost her heart to her as quickly as I had.

In those two weeks, I realized that the actual "work" of Pepper was not all that time consuming, nor demanding. It was my brain that made the situation feel overwhelming to me, and made my chest collapse like a deflated balloon.

Pepper---and every other little or big task in my life---was an indicator to me of the way my brain constructs the frame of my feelings, and how it overlays that framing onto my body: If my brain tells me I am rushed and overwhelmed, and then my body follows right along and gets tired and anxious. But it really all starts with the thought. If I can capture that thought for a moment and release it from my body, I feel better.

What could I do about this revelation? The same thing my gardening friend Keith did when asked what he was going to do about the horde of flea beetles munching on his potato plants.

"I'm going to watch them," he said.

So I watched where my mind went with Pepper. The thought of her care some days seemed overwhelming to me, and yet when I had my hands on her actually giving her care, the moments were magic---almost sacred. Trying to figure it all out was not the way for me to go about this. It never is. Watching it, watching the thoughts and feelings, was and remains the wiser way. Insights arise naturally from this kind of processing.

A couple days passed with Pepper refusing her food. I watched the thought about her not eating assail me throughout the day. My breathing went shallow. My shoulders hunched. So I took long breaths and said to myself, "She'll eat more when she is ready. Bigger hands than yours are in charge of the outcome here. Your task is simply to love and to offer supportive care." And those comforting words from my heart to my brain helped my shoulders to square themselves and my breathing to deepen. And of course, Pepper returned happily to her food bowl.

One day, I cleaned out the old empty chicken coop and filled it deeply with fresh straw. I put a small wooden dog house at the far end, set a bowl of water in the corner, and moved Pepper out of her bucket to the secure enclosure. In the chicken coop, she would have room to move if she ever wanted to. Meanwhile, she'd have the familiar healing sounds of nature all around her.

The following morning, I found her cuddled like a half-moon in the straw next to the doghouse. Too hot for sleeping in the little wooden house, I figured. At the far end of the coop was a small pile of droppings. In the night, Pepper had roamed her new territory, pooping as far away from her sleeping quarters as possible.

I woke her up the way I always do: With a stroke of her head and a syringe of cherry flavored medicine at her nose. She yawned and shook her head as if to work the cobwebs out of her brain. I picked her up and cradled her like a baby and cooed to her, stroking the top of her forehead with my fingers. I've always sensed she liked this position. She yawned again and looked up into my face, and I saw that---for the first time---there was someone home inside that little head. Since I brought her home, she as been a willing patient, accepting all that comes to her with a blank, quiet resolve. She was quiet on this morning, too, but it was a different kind of quiet. It seemed to me that some of her soul had returned to her body to light up her eyes. She stretched her funny bowlegs out to encourage me to rub her tummy---the first overture she had ever made to me. With her soft front paws, she held my finger and looked deeply into my eyes, never blinking. My own vision grew blurred.

What happened next was totally unexpected. After more than three months of caring for Pepper and watching her take her small but steady steps toward recovery, I no longer expected Pepper to die. We'd been spending evenings with her curled in my lap by the TV where I'd stroke her gently and whisper to her in baby talk. She would look at me with those black-buttons eyes and respond in her own special way, usually by sighing, yawning, or washing her face and tail---and just as often my fingers.

The end began one evening as I was holding her---as usual---and she was behaving nothing like usual. Her body was tense. She did not yawn, she did not once clean her sweet face. She tried to hide her head under my elbow and her body felt tense and stiff.

I don't know why her sudden change in behavior that evening passed over me without setting off any alarm inside my head. I turned to Carter and said, "She's not wanting this attention anymore. I think she's coming back to her wild self."

"That's good," he answered and smiled. "It means she must be feeling better all the time."

When I carried her back to her chicken coop that night, she fought to get out of my arms and trundled clumsily into her hutch. "I'm sorry Pepper," I whispered to her. "I didn't listen to you earlier. Cuddling is something I still want, but you no longer need. I'll give you your space, little girl."

Next morning, Pepper's food dish sat untouched. She hadn't eaten anything in two days.

Finally, the alarm bells sounded. I picked her up and hurried her indoors and set her on the carpet. My heart skipped when I saw she could no longer move her front legs in any way but to push away from herself. She only looked in one direction. Her back legs had no coordination at all. Stricken, I cradled her to me baby-fashion, something she had always enjoyed. She gripped my fingers hard with her front paws. Then, she sighed and went limp and relaxed in my arms. Suddenly, I realized that her eyes were pulsing back and forth, back and forth. My breath caught in my throat. Pepper was not returning to her wild self at all. She was having small seizures, a string of them, back to back. Now I knew why she hadn't eaten. She didn't eat because she could not keep her face in the dish. It kept jerking out. And I knew, also, why she acted as though she were pushing me away the night before. Her front arms were going rigid in a repetitive motion.

I put her in a carrier and raced off to WildCare. I wanted others at the center to see Pepper and to give me their own take on what was happening to her, and why. My plan was to get Pepper to our wildlife veterinarian for evaluation. I was planning to stop for lunch with a friend first, but of course that never happened. I imagined that Pepper would be examined, given tests and more medicine, and that we would keep traveling the healing journey together. But somewhere in the course of the next two hours, I would see the situation differently.

Pepper was suffering. How many more hours or days of this could she take? After talks, consults, and tears, I chose euthanasia for her as the kindest, most responsible act on her behalf. Possums have a very slow metabolism, and seem to absorb certain medications slower than many other mammals.

For Pepper, it meant that she would take nearly an hour to expire in my arms.

It was a profound, gentle hour, during which a tender peace wrapped itself around both of us. Pepper returned to herself again as the drugs kicked in, breathing calmly, yawning, and licking her paws and my fingers. When death called her, she left with a contented sigh.

I have loved and lost many animals in my time. Probably owing to the antidepressants I take, I find that grief over these wildlife losses passes blessedly quickly for me these days. I believe without question that animals do not particularly care if they are in the body or out of it. Their spirits are far more connected to universal consciousness, or God, than we humans, and they can access this connection in or out of physical body. What remains for me in the loss is a usually non-conflicted sadness and loneliness at their passing.

And so I my reaction to losing Pepper came as unexpectedly as her death. I was devastated, and remained so for many weeks. I reflected on the meaning of her coming to me, and leaving me, and found myself missing her more instead of less as the days passed. Yes, I knew she was a teacher for me. But I had no idea how deep her lessons went.

I could not refrain from looking at old photos of her, or stopping in the middle of a day to go sit in the chicken coop where she lived, just to sit with her memory. I'd replay her passing in my mind and chide myself for choosing euthanasia. But then I remember her terrified eyes and spastic body, and know in my bones I made the right choice. Right choice or not, I could not yet find myself a path across the void she left in my heart. When I had found Pepper sick and dying in an old leaf pile, I believed she had come to me for comfort and healing. What I find in truth is that she came to me for my own comfort and healing. Many are the ways she touched me in her short life, but many more are the ways she is reaching out to me in her death.

Ever so gently the summer took her leave from the Enchanted Forest where I live. She packed away her most blistering hot days and humid nights. A few trees were trying on some fall color. Nothing overdone, really, just a few splashy accessories. Autumn is the winsome, looking-back time for me. A season when I take stock of my summer's accomplishments, or lack of them. Pepper's death came on the very heels of the summer's retreat, and so my reflections on my time with her coincided exactly with the sense of wistful melancholy that always touches me on the shoulders come autumn.

The first crisp mornings of summer's end found me thinking deeply about Pepper---about who she was, and what she meant in the riddle of my own life. I often refer to my animal symbol guidebooks for insight, and for a kind of spring-board into personal explorations. In Jamie Sams' "Animal Medicine Cards," two symbolic "gifts" of Opossum that struck me most at first reflection were "expect the unexpected," and "sometimes the best defense is no defense at all." Possums are renowned for their ability to play dead. Actually, they play more than dead. They play decomposing. A possum playing dead stinks like you would not believe. Predators will often back off, surprised and repelled, at the site and stench of an opossum going into a death trance. And the possum wakes up later, shakes itself off, and wanders---safe---into the woods. It occurred to me that depression is like living half-dead, like a possum in a near-death trance, but without the stench.

In reading more about opossums, I also have discovered that they are the poster children for early onset senescence, or aging. When I first found Pepper, I had thought of her as a youngster with her first litter of joeys. But her teeth revealed she was at least a year old, probably a bit more. In the wild, a possum usually survives only a year or two at best. And not just because of circumstances. A three-year-old possum looks as rickety as an ancient old crone: grey, stiff jointed, stained fur, missing or broken yellowed teeth and claws. I've seen some that even seem to have the palsy of the very old.

I, too, suffer from my own brand of senescence. I am

aging quickly---too quickly I believe---and struggling with medical issues faced mostly by those far older than I. By coincidence or providence, Pepper placed herself in my path. Pepper, a creature strongly identified by her unique relationship to aging. I ask myself, did I draw her to me to mirror my issues with growing old too quickly, or was she sent to bring a message about my relationship to aging that I need to ponder? Was Pepper a model, an example, a message, or all and none of these?

I'm inclined to believe that she was all of these, plus--- most importantly---she was herself, a creature with dignity making her way and doing her best in the few short years the universe grants to opossums.

There are ways to forestall "aging," these days: supplements, Botox, surgery, affirmations, stress reduction, diet, pills. I am out putting my hands in my pond to pull out the end-of-summer, yellowed pond plants when the thought strikes me: Age stalks us all like a coyote on a rabbit scent. "Sometimes the best defense is no defense at all..." Suddenly, I thought of Pepper and grinned.

Was it a celestial choir kind of moment? Did the clouds part to reveal the face of God? No. It was just me smiling with my hands in my cold pond, and my thoughts on a gentle, rickety possum and on the gentle, rickety softness of my own crone body, riddled with its aches, pains, and chronic melancholy. There was nothing to defend myself against in that moment. And there was nothing to do but---as my friend Keith reminds me---simply watch.

The pond plants felt slippery in my fingers, like newborn infants. I have held wet, squirming newborns of many kinds in my hands, feeling the intimacy of new life, as I had held Pepper's dying infants in my palm, feeling the sadness of fresh promise never realized. No skies parted with shafts of gold beaming down upon me. But a question shook my world tenderly from the inside out, sparking a healing not yet born in me but---thanks to Pepper---on its way.

What if I could wean myself from the anti-depressants?

Who would I be now with my feeling world unshackled by the merciless heaviness of drug sedation? Am I depressed because of the medications? Who knows? How might it feel to feel again?

Tentatively, I have begun the process. The sleeping pills are gone now. The anti-depressants sit by my bedside should I begin a slide back into the black hole and need them. I tell myself, even if I can feel myself for only a week or two before I need to go back on the meds, how amazing would that be--- to feel myself---to feel who I am twenty years since I last remember being un-numbed?

"Expect the Unexpected..." I pass by the chicken coop that was Pepper's last home and put a vase of fading flowers at the door. I decide to rename the chicken coop "Pepper's House." And suddenly my throat chokes up and the pain of her loss feels to me like paradise: My heart awakening to the wrenching exquisiteness of a real, unencumbered, un-blanketed feeling. I remember the look of Pepper with her long, silly possum nose, doddering across the dining room carpet on those precious days when her four legs would actually work as they should. I remember how she opened herself to me, unguarded and defenseless in her need. For a moment, I raise one hand up to the sky, sending a brief prayer that I may walk as openly, as fearlessly, and as undefended into the simple mystery of my life.

(Susan Chernak McElroy is the author of *Animals as Teachers and Healers.*)

4 SUNSHINE: I LOVE YOU, SWEET BABY
by Allen and Linda Anderson

"If we raised our voices or exchanged harsh words, the tense moment would dissolve into laughter or astonishment, as Sunshine sang HU from the wooden perch in his cage. The sweet warble of his chanting would remind us that nothing is more important, no argument too heated, no need to be right too strong that it can't dissolve into the ocean of love within the sound of HU."

They didn't have parrot personalities, extensive vocabularies, or the precise ability to imitate human voices. Yet Sunshine and Sparkle, cute and tiny cockatiels, took over our living room and our lives from the moment we brought them home.

Sunshine, his yellow feathers and bright orange cheeks fluffed, swaggered with male energy and an overload of testosterone. When he was younger, he began to imitate sounds he heard in his home. We would gently place him on our living room fireplace mantel, which had a mirror fixed to the wall behind it. There, Sunshine demonstrated his male ego. He'd gaze at his beautiful body and say, "I love you, sweet baby." Then he'd make the kissing sound he had heard his humans direct toward him. Occasionally he'd offer his expression of endearment to Linda too. But never to Allen. It was a guy thing.

Through the first twelve years of Sunshine's life, he lived

with our yellow Labrador retriever Taylor, who along with our two cats, was a bird's natural predator. We only let the birds out of their spacious cage for a stroll on the mantel, to waddle around the living room, or to sit on our shoulders while Taylor and the cats were sequestered in other parts of the house.

One time, Allen took Sunshine and Sparkle, our tiny gray female who also sported bright orange cheeks, to the mantel. Allen had forgotten that our rambunctious puppy was roaming around. After working for a while in his office, he returned to the living room and found dog and bird, nose to beak. Sunshine had flown to the floor, where he and Taylor curiously checked each other out.

Perhaps in an attempt to form a fast friendship, Sunshine was saying to Taylor, "Hello." Allen swooped the little adventurer out of harm's way before Taylor tried to paw the bird into a delightful new toy. Sparkle wisely had stayed on the mantel. Allen had to sit on the couch for a few minutes and recover from the emotions of averting a near disaster.

Sunshine and Taylor's relationship evolved into a playful relationship. Taylor adored Allen, and the sound of his voice whistling for her to come to him made her tremble with happiness. Sometimes, when we let Taylor outside on the deck and in the backyard, Sunshine and Sparkle would be having their mantel-walking time.

A small screened-in window next to the mantle overlooked the deck. This is where we would find Sunshine peeking out and imitating Allen's whistle. Taylor would bound onto the deck, eagerly anticipating a reunion with her best friend in the world. At the panting sound of Taylor's arrival, her front paws scratching the windowsill, and her big tail thumping on the red wooden deck, Sunshine would scurry to the other end of the mantel and hide his identity as the "whistleblower." After Taylor gave up and returned to the backyard, Sunshine waited for a respectable amount of time and then started the game all over again until one of us brought her inside.

Sunshine didn't reserve his practical jokes only for the dog. When he felt certain that Allen was outside mowing the lawn or Linda was downstairs doing the laundry, his other favorite game was to make the sound of the phone ring. He imitated the ringing so perfectly that one or both of us would come running to answer it. As soon our shrewd trickster saw a hand poised to pick up the phone, with perfect timing, he said, "hello!"

Linda enjoyed challenging Sunshine's creative intellect by making up tunes or whistling the melodies to songs. He could whistle back the chorus to "This Old Man" and "When the Saints Go Marching In." Remarkably he would listen to a short composition of Linda's in the morning, think about it all day, and then whistle it, note-for-note, the next morning. Not content to merely "parrot" the melodies, he composed variations. Linda would repeat his compositions by whistling them back but she could never keep up with his improvised notes and trills. In the battle of dueling whistlers, Sunshine was definitely the winner.

Even though he tended to be somewhat of a curmudgeon – quick with the open beak and sharply biting human fingers – Sunshine had a spiritual side to his nature. Linda and Allen both sing an ancient chant called HU (spelled capital HU and pronounced like the word hue) as part of their spiritual practice each morning. This holy love song to God, a way of calming stress and connecting to the Life Force within all creation, appealed to Sunshine.

If we raised our voices or exchanged harsh words, the tense moment would dissolve into laughter or astonishment, as Sunshine sang HU from the wooden perch in his cage. The sweet warble of his chanting would remind us that nothing is more important, no argument too heated, no need to be right too strong that it can't dissolve into the ocean of love within the sound of HU.

Because we write books about the spiritual partnerships between people and animals, the uniqueness of our mission caught the attention of a religion reporter at the Minneapolis

Star Tribune newspaper. Martha came over to our house to interview us about our Angel Animals Network and to meet our animal companions. As we spoke to her about pet family members and our desire to bring more love into the world by sharing stories about human-animal spiritual connection, she took notes. Martha also ran a tape recorder that she placed on the living room table.

From his cage in the corner of the living room, Sunshine watched the interview. (Everything that happened in the living room served as his private entertainment.) Occasionally as we spoke with Martha, he would chime in with a chirp or whistle.

Later that week, Martha called us to verify quotes. She said that when she listened to her tape recording, each time the interview veered into discussing a spiritual subject, Sunshine would join in the conversation. When we talked about other things, he remained silent. She was impressed by our wise little bird's interest in spiritual topics. She said, "Sunshine is truly an Angel Animal, isn't he?" We agreed.

Sparkle was much smaller and more delicate than Sunshine. She would sit on Linda's lap and move her head around while Linda finger-massaged the little bird's neck. Sparkle loved to take rides on Linda's and Allen's shoulders, accompanying them to the kitchen to wash dishes, to the bedroom to make the bed, or to their offices where she supervised their writing and listened to them tapping on computer keyboards. While perched on their shoulders, Sunshine groomed their hair with her beak, just as she did every day on the mantel for her beloved.

Sparkle needed breaks from the amorous Sunshine. His testosterone-fueled lovemaking was wearing her out. The avian veterinarian explained that in order for Sparkle to stop producing so many eggs, some of which became impacted, we would have to give her a separate cage from Sunshine. Even after they each had their own space, though, his manly presence continued to make her hormones surge.

The vet showed Linda how to hold this tiny bird in one

hand and give her hormone injections with the other. The hope was that the injections would help our lovesick bird lay off the egg-laying. But clearly, by the time she was about six years old, Sparkle's body, already more fragile than Sunshine's, grew progressively weaker.

One morning, after Sparkles's many bouts with illness, medications, and vet visits, we found her lifeless body on the floor of the cage. Her devoted mate repeatedly circled the love of his life. With a sound we had never heard before or since, Sunshine emitted a mournful cry, like Irish keening at a wake. For hours, Sunshine continued his funeral ritual. He nudged Sparkle with is beak, pleading with her to come back to him.

Should we remove Sparkle from the cage? we wondered. We decided to take our cues from Sunshine. He continued his grief-stricken vigil for eight hours. Finally he left his sweetheart, climbed the ladder to his favorite perch, and looked down on his dear companion.

"Sunshine, are you ready for us to take Sparkle outside?" we asked him. He turned his head and looked away from her. "We are going to bury her and have a memorial service," we assured him feebly. He gazed at us blankly, still in shock over Sparkle's passing. Then he turned his head from us as if to say, "Go ahead. I know that she is gone now."

For many weeks after Sparkle's death, we gave Sunshine extra attention. We whistled to him and repeated his favorite "I love you, sweet baby" words. We took him to the mantel, where he and Sparkle used to share their seed bowl and groom each other. Sunshine would walk to the edge of the mantel and stare out the window. *Is she coming back?* he seemed to be asking.

After a couple of weeks, he began to sing and whistle back to us. One day, he flew from the mantel for his customary ride on Linda's shoulder. That's when we knew things were getting back to some normalcy for him.

Throughout Sunshine's mourning period, we spoke to him about the gray cockatiel we all missed. "Sparkle was special. She was so pretty. She loved you. She still loves you."

These were human words of comfort. He didn't need them. He had his own proof. We watched him looking past us and over our heads. He followed the invisible flight of his mate as her spirit body flew to join him on the mantel. He looked for his Sparkle each day and for several months after the death of her physical body and found her presence in a way that only he could see and experience.

We wondered if we should find another mate for Sunshine. Each time we talked about the idea, we got the impression that this is not what he wanted. Eventually he came to enjoy being an only child who got all the attention. From his perch, our changing family of cats and dogs provided him with hours of amusement and fascination.

Now that Sunshine is a senior citizen in his twenties, he's still a feisty composer and whistler of his own tunes. He still makes the kissing sound to Linda (not to Allen). It has been many years since his Sparkle went ahead of him to the inner worlds. He has never again said to the birdie in the mirror or to anyone else: "I love you, sweet baby." He seems to be waiting for the right time, when two special souls reunite, to tell Sparkle how he feels, how he has always felt. (Allen and Linda Anderson have published 15 books including *A Dog Named Leaf: The Hero from Heaven Who Saved My Life.*)

5 SMUDGE: THANK YOU FOR BEING MY TEACHER
by Bernie Siegel, M. D.

"Because I had done something that led to her suffering she was not going to do something that would lead to my suffering. She showed me that we humans can also choose to love and not be like the people who hurt us. To put it simply she taught me about love with that simple gesture and how complete animals are while man struggles to become complete. She showed me how curses can become blessings which help us to grow and how to love the unlovable, forgive the unforgivable and become free."

Several years ago I was going through a difficult time because someone in our cancer support group I had known for many years was not taking proper care of herself. Being a physician, I was very upset with her for not taking her medications and vitamins and I was becoming angry at her for not loving herself as much as I loved her. I was constantly asking her if she had taken her medications, exercised and more. Our conversations were not about what we appreciated about life but what she hadn't done right. The only thing my anger was accomplishing was ruining our relationship.

She began to avoid me but I found it very hard to not be critical of someone who was not doing the best thing for herself and seeing her life as a gift to be cared for. This is something I have learned from the people I counsel with life threatening illnesses who are grateful for every day, and here she was not living the sermon.

During this time my wife, Bobbie, and I were glancing out the sunroom window at our goldfish pond when two little rabbits appeared. One was pure white and the other black. These obviously abandoned Easter bunnies were not going to survive for long in the wooded area we live in. They wouldn't let us approach them so we set out a trap which closes behind the animal when it enters to eat the food in the trap. The next morning the black bunny, which my wife named Smudge, was safe inside. The white bunny was never seen again, probably because her color made it hard for her to escape predators.

I built a four room bungalow in our enclosed front yard for Smudge and she shared the yard with our four cats. They became family and as I began to read more about rabbits and see how intelligent and loving Smudge was, she became a house rabbit. She had her space in the kitchen where all her needs were met and her days were spent in the front yard or lounging in her apartment.

Things went well for our five four-legged children, and then one day I came home with a little abandoned Lhasa Apso I rescued from the local animal shelter. Bobbie said we already had enough furphies all over the house, meaning bits of fur. So I named him Furphy and he became a family member too. Our problems began when Bobbie and I went shopping one day and I forgot to close the pet door to the front yard. I thought of it after we left the house but decided Smudge would be safe since Furphy and she were acquainted with each other. However, Furphy went out into the yard while we were away and he must have thought Smudge was similar to a stuffed toy because he grabbed her and injured her. I felt enormous guilt because I had forgotten to close the pet door.

I am a surgeon so I cleaned her wounds and then I took her to the veterinarian where I learned that rabbits were considered exotic pets and not all veterinarians were familiar with their medical needs and care. She underwent surgery and I became her caregiver at home, dressing her wounds, medicating and feeding her. She became my teacher. Each morning and evening I would medicate her and care for her wounds.

While dressing her wounds if I did anything that hurt, she did not become aggressive or try to run away. Rather, she would turn her head and lick my hand. Something no patient had ever done. We were family and despite my inadequacies, she accepted me and loved me. Because I had done something that led to her suffering she was not going to do something that would lead to my suffering. She showed me that we humans can also choose to love and not be like the people who hurt us. To put it simply she taught me about love with that simple gesture and how complete animals are while man struggles to become complete. She showed me how curses can become blessings which help us to grow and how to love the unlovable, forgive the unforgivable and become free.

Caring for Smudge involved my time for several months. As her wounds healed and she no longer required medications and special meals she was able to return to her normal routine. One evening, I went out in the yard to bring her into the house, which she never liked to do, so she ran and hid behind Furphy. In that moment, I saw how Furphy had been forgiven and was now acting as her guardian, helping her to remain outdoors and not spend her time in the kitchen. Evenings the two of them would nestle in the living room with Bobbie and me and the cats to watch TV. We were family and as one of our children said, "The animals get along better than people because they're all the same color inside." As a surgeon I realize that that statement is true for all of us and perhaps one day we will become one family and be as complete as the animals are.

In honor of Smudge and her difficult life I helped the local animal shelter establish a rabbit rescue. We have a cabin called Smudge's place and take in abandoned rabbits. I painted a picture for it showing Peter Rabbit's Mom dressing her children and above them are the words Smudge's Place.

Many lives have been saved in Smudge's name.

What I learned from her was that blessings come in many forms. Some are painful and even life threatening but if they help us to become more complete human beings then they truly are blessings. The Bible tells us that everything God created God saw was good but when God created man that word was not used. A Rabbi said the word in Hebrew was Tov and that the meaning of the word "good" has been lost because we use it so frequently. It is better interpreted as complete. I can honestly say that Smudge and all our animals have helped me become a more complete human being. They taught me that love is blind because it does not see the faults of the other person.

They have also taught me to live in the moment as they do. Not fearing tomorrow or regretting yesterday but enjoying today and the opportunities it provides us with. They appreciate their bodies and do not complain about them. As a veterinarian who was about to undergo surgery said, "I can amputate a leg or a jaw and they wake up and lick their owners faces. They are here to love and be loved and teach us a few things."

I have learned from Smudge to love, forgive and be merciful towards an individual even when I do not like what they have done. Through understanding I have found the antidote to hate and when I do not hate I am capable of loving and achieving justice for all involved. If we each treated ourselves and others as we do our beloved pets we would all live longer healthier lives. Nine hundred years ago Maimonides, the Jewish physician and philosopher wrote, "If people would take as good care of themselves as they do their animals they would suffer fewer illnesses."

Smudge helped me to realize that only when I love other people and help them to love themselves does healing occur. I now know I can reparent those who do not care about themselves and through my love help them to accept themselves and begin to care for themselves through their feelings of self-worth and self-love. I have seen this happen with suicidal patients whom I have loved and family members too. Rather than criticize I love until they can accept that they are worth loving and change their behavior. Then my criticism polishes their mirror and is constructive because they know it comes from someone who loves them. As one suicidal young woman said to me, "You are my CD. My Chosen Dad."

Having been born an ugly duckling I know what it is like to have a grandmother who could love me unconditionally when my parents were trying to hide me from people so as not to upset them. The ugly duckling did a rare thing. He looked at his reflection and saw a swan. Something most of us could not accomplish on our own. I could look into my grandmother's eyes as a child or Smudge's eyes now, and see in their gaze that I was a swan.

6 JETHRO: AMBASSADOR OF FRIENDSHIP AND COMPASSION
By Dr. Marc Bekoff

"Dogs trust us almost unconditionally. It's great to be trusted and loved, and no one does it better than dogs. Jethro was no exception. But along with trust and love come many serious responsibilities and difficult moral choices. I find it easiest to think about dog trust in terms of what they expect from us. They have great faith in us; they expect we'll always have their best interests in mind, that we'll care for them and make them as happy as we can. Indeed, we welcome them into our homes as family members who bring us much joy and deep friendship."

Jethro, my companion dog for nearly a decade, came into my life when I met him at the local humane society. He was about nine months old and looked to be part Rotweiler, part German shepherd, with little bit of hound thrown into his gene pool. He was black and tan, somewhat barrel-chested, with dripping jowls and long floppy ears. Jethro was low-key, gentle, and well-mannered. He did not chase other animals around my mountain home. He just loved to hang out and watch the world around him. He made a perfect field assistant for me as I was studying various birds living around my house.

One day, while I was sitting inside, I heard Jethro come to the front door. Instead of whining as he usually did when he wanted to come in, he just sat there. I looked at him and noticed a small furry object in his mouth. My first reaction was "Oh no, he killed a bird." However, when I opened the door, Jethro proceeded to drop a very young bunny at my feet- drenched in his saliva - who was still moving. I could not see any injuries - just a small bundle of fur who needed warmth, food, and love.

Jethro looked up at me, wide-eyed, as if he wanted me to praise him for being such a good Samaritan. I did. He was so proud of his compassionate self. I guessed that the bunny's mother had disappeared - most likely she fell prey to a coyote, red fox, and the occasional mountain lion around my house.

When I picked the bunny up Jethro got very concerned. He tried to snatch her from my hands, whined, and followed me around as I gathered a box, a blanket, and some water and food. I gently placed the bunny in the box, named her "Bunny," and wrapped her in the blanket. After a while I put some mashed up carrots, celery, and lettuce near her and she tried to eat. I also made sure that she knew where the water was.

All the while, Jethro was standing behind me, panting, dripping saliva on my shoulder, and watching my every move. I thought he would go for Bunny or the food, but rather he stood there, fascinated by this little ball of fur slowly moving about in her new home.

When I had to leave the box, I called Jethro but he simply would not leave. He usually came to me immediately, especially when I offered him a bone, but he steadfastly remained near the box for hours on end.

Finally, I had to drag Jethro out to give him his nightly walk. When we returned he bee-lined for the box and that is where he slept through the night. I tried to get Jethro to go to his usual sleeping spot and he refused.

"No way," he said, "I am staying here." I trusted Jethro not to harm Bunny and he did not during the two weeks. I nursed her back to health so that I could release her near my house. Jethro had adopted Bunny – he was her friend. He would make sure that no one harmed Bunny.

Finally, the day came when I introduced Bunny to the outdoors. Jethro and I walked to the east side of my house and I released her from her box and watched her slowly make her way into a woodpile. She was cautious - her senses were overwhelmed by the new stimuli - sights, sounds, and odors - to which she was now exposed.

Bunny remained in the woodpile for about an hour until she boldly stepped out to begin life as a full-fledged rabbit. Jethro remained where he had laid down and watched the whole scenario. He never took his eyes off of Bunny and never tried to approach her or to snatch her.

Bunny hung around for a few months. Every time I let Jethro out of the house he immediately ran to the spot where she was released. When he arrived there he would cock his head and move it from side-to-side, looking for Bunny. This lasted for about six months! When I would utter Bunny in a high-pitched voice, Jethro would whine and go look for her. Bunny was his friend and he was hoping to see her once again.

I am not sure what happened to Bunny. Other bunnies and adults rabbits have come and gone, and Jethro looks at each of them, perhaps wondering if they are Bunny. He tries to get as close as he can. He never chases them.

I think Jethro is a truly compassionate soul. Last summer, nine years after he met Bunny and treated her with delicate compassion, he came running up to me with a wet animal in his mouth. Hmm, I wondered, another bunny? I asked him to drop it and he did. This time it was a young bird who had flown into a window. It was stunned and just needed to gain its senses. I held it in my hands for a few minutes. Jethro, in true fashion, watched my and the bird's every move. When I thought it was ready to fly I placed the bird on the railing of my porch. Jethro approached it, sniffed it, stepped back, and watched it fly away.

Jethro has saved two animals from death. He could easily have gulped each down with little effort. But you don't do that to friends, do you?

"Come on Marc, it's time for a hike, or dinner, or a belly rub." I shared my home for 12 years with my friend, and even though I had rescued Jethro from the Humane Society in Boulder, in many ways he had rescued me. As he got older, it became clear that our lives together soon would be over. The uninhibited and exuberant wagging of his whip-like tail, which fanned me in the summer, occasionally knocked glasses off the table, and told me how happy he was, would soon stop.

What should I do? Let him live in misery or help him die peacefully, with dignity? It was my call and a hard one at that. But just as I was there for him in life, I needed to be there for him as he approached death, to·put his interests before mine, to help end his suffering, to help him cross into his mysterious future with grace, dignity, and love. For sure, easier said than done.

Dogs trust us almost unconditionally. It's great to be trusted and loved, and no one does it better than dogs. Jethro was no exception. But along with trust and love come many serious responsibilities and difficult moral choices. I find it easiest to think about dog trust in terms of what they expect from us. They have great faith in us; they expect we'll always have their best interests in mind, that we'll care for them and make them as happy as we can. Indeed, we welcome them into our homes as family members who bring us much joy and deep friendship.

Because they're so dependent on us, we're also responsible for making difficult decisions about when to end their lives, to "put them to sleep. "I've been faced with this situation many times and have anguished trying to "do what's right" for my buddies. Should I let them live a bit longer or has the time really come to say good-bye?

When Jethro got old and could hardly walk, eat, or hold his water, the time had come for me to put him out of his misery. He was dying right in front of my eyes and in my heart, I knew it. Even when eating a bagel, he was miserable. Deciding when to end an animal's life is a real-life moral drama. There aren't any dress rehearsals and doing it once doesn't make doing it again any easier.

Jethro knew I'd do what's best for him and I really came to feel that often he'd look at me and say, "It's okay, please take me out of my misery and lessen your burden. Let me have a dignified ending to what was a great life. Neither of us feels better letting me go on like this. "Finally, I chose to let Jethro leave Earth in peace.

After countless hugs and "I love you's," to this day I swear that Jethro knew what was happening, when he went for his last car ride, something he loved to do, and that he accepted his fate with valor, grace, and honor. And I feel heal so told me that the moral dilemma with which I was faced was no predicament at all, that I had indeed done all I could and that his trust in me was not compromised one bit, but, perhaps, strengthened. I made the right choice and he openly thanked us for it. And he wished me well, and assured me that I could go on with no remorse or apologies. Let's thank our animal companions for who they are. Let's rejoice and embrace them as the amazing beings they are. If we open our hearts to them we can learn much from their selfless lessons in compassion, humility, generosity, kindness, devotion, respect, spirituality, and love.

By honoring our dogs' trust we tap into our own spirituality, into our hearts and souls. And sometimes that means not only killing them with love, but also mercifully taking their lives when their own spirit has died and life's flame has been irreversibly extinguished. Our companions are counting on us to be for them in all situations, to let them go and not to let their lives deteriorate into base, undignified humiliation while we ponder our own needs in lieu of theirs. We are obliged to do so. We can do no less.

7 JASPER: SPOKESBEAR FOR FORGIVENESS, TRUST, AND HOPE
by Dr. Marc Bekoff

"As an ethologist, I always want to learn more about each being as an individual, what they feel, how they travel through life, and how they keep their dreams alive.

I wonder what Jasper and other moon bears carry in their head - what remnants of unspeakable abuse and trauma remain. Perhaps they also talk about how lucky they are to have been rescued and that not all humans are bad, that they can trust some of us."

Jasper arrived at the Moon Bear Rescue Centre outside of Chengdu, China in 2000 and given the name he proudly carries. Jill Robinson MBE (founder of Animals Asia) and the wonderful humans who work with her receive bears from bear farms after the bears are no longer useful to the farmers. Bears usually arrive in horrible condition, suffering from serious physical and psychological trauma. Each bear is given a complete physical and a psychological evaluation. Many need surgery because of their physical condition (missing paws, worn down teeth, or liver cancer). After they've acclimated to the center some bears have to be kept alone, whereas others can be introduced to other bears.

For fifteen years Jasper's home was a tiny, filthy "crush

cage" in which he couldn't move on a bear farm in China. Jasper was continually squashed to the bottom of his filthy cage to squeeze out his bile. Imagine being pinned in a phone booth for even fifteen minutes and all you could do was turn your head to drink water and eat. As if this wasn't enough, Jasper also had a rusty metal catheter inserted into his gall bladder so that his bile could be collected to treat various ailments in the spurious name of traditional Chinese medicine. Despite it all, Jasper survived.

When I first met Jasper he immediately reminded me of Jethro - kind and gentle with big brown eyes that stared right into my heart. Each had a tan stripe across his chest; for Jasper the tan crescent is the reason he's called a moon bear. I'm sure it was Jasper's and Jethro's optimistic spirit and trust that's allowed them to thrive. At the Humane Society, Jethro had the reputation for liking all the other animals, including the ducks, geese, and goats he occasionally met in the outdoor run. Jethro came home with me, kept me happy and healthy, rescued injured birds and bunnies around my mountain home, and taught me many important life lessons. Jasper's and Jethro's spiritual path is as an inspirational lesson for how we can all be healthy, alive, and connected, and recover from untold and unimaginable trauma. Each of these individuals also displayed unbounded empathy for others.

When I first saw Jasper I could feel his gentle kindness-- the same for Jethro. Their omniscient eyes say, "All's well, the past is past, let go and move on." Jasper's gait was slow and smooth as he approached me as I fed him peaches out of a bucket. I then gave Jasper peanut butter and his long and wiry tongue glided out of his mouth and he gently lapped the tasty treat from my fingers. Jill Robinson best describes Jasper's softness, his kind disposition: "Touching the back of his paw one day I saw his head turn towards me, soft brown eyes blinking with trust and I knew that Jasper was going to be a special friend."

Jasper knew that things were going to get better and that he would recover. Jasper tells people and other bears, "All will be okay, trust me." Likewise, when I was having a bad day, Jethro also reminded me to look on the bright side of things. When Jasper was finally released from his recovery cage at the rescue centre he was delighted to be free. Jill watched him approach a bear on the other side of the bars separating them and reach out as if to shake paws with the stranger who was to become his best friend. The other bear, Delaney, (nicknamed Aussie) sniffed Jasper's paw and then put his paws through the bars so that Jasper could return the favor. Jasper and Aussie remain close friends and I've had the pleasure -- I might say a delightful treat and honor -- of watching them play, rest together, and perhaps share stories of the their horrible pasts and the wonderful humans with whom they're lucky to live with now. Many of the bears love to play, and this is an indication that they've substantially recovered from their trauma.

When I visited the Moon Bear Rescue center in October 2008 I saw Aussie and Frank frolicking on a hammock. They were having a great time and it was incredibly inspiring to see these bears enjoying life. Jill and I shared their joy as we laughed at their silly antics. When Aussie saw Jasper ambling over he jumped off the hammock, approached Jasper, and they began roughhousing - caressing one another, biting one another's scruff and ears, and falling to the ground embracing and rolling around. After a while Jasper went over to a water hole and invited Aussie in but Aussie decided to stay on the shore and watch Jasper play in the water. Tears came to my eyes. Not only were these bears telling one another that the day was going just fine but they were also telling Jill and me that all was okay. Much of the deep trauma that they'd experienced was in the past and whatever lingered wasn't stopping them from enjoying themselves and spreading joy to other bears. Traumatized animals don't play and surely aren't as out-going as these awesome bears.

Jasper remains the peacemaker. He makes other bears feel at ease and that's how I felt when I first met him. Perhaps Jasper knows what the other bears have experienced and wants to reassure them that everything will be okay now that they've been rescued. Jasper truly opens up his heart to everyone he meets. And, I think Jasper knows the effect he has on others. Jill told me that at a social function to celebrate their recent book Freedom Moon (Jasper stole the show. He always does - and he knows it. But there's no arrogance at all - just trust and confidence that all is well and will continue to be so.)

If one didn't know what Jasper had experienced they'd never guess for it isn't apparent from his behavior and spirit. Are Jasper and a few others special, and if so, why? Why did they recover and others didn't? Bears, like dogs and other animals, display different personalities. Big Aussie still runs back into his den when he hears a strange noise or even when he sees a caterpillar in the grass. As an ethologist, I always want to learn more about each being as an individual, what they feel, how they travel through life, and how they keep their dreams alive.

I wonder what Jasper, Aussie, and other moon bears carry in their head - what remnants of unspeakable abuse and trauma remain. Perhaps they also talk about how lucky they are to have been rescued and that not all humans are bad, that they can trust some of us. Many of the bears have been able to get over a lot of what they experienced, at least overtly, and depend on the trust, loyalty, and love that they've developed over time with the same mammalian species - human beings - who couldn't care less about their well-being.

Jasper is the spokes-bear for forgiveness, peace, trust, and hope. I can't thank Jasper enough for sharing his journey and his dreams. Jasper, like the dogs and cats who also need us, make us more humane and thus more human. The true spirit of humans, our inborn nature, is to help rather than to harm.

These stories are excerpts from *The Smile of a Dolphin* (New Age Library) and Dr. Bekoff's article, *Animal Emotions,* on *The Psychology Today* www.psychologytoday.com/basics/mating

8 ARE YOU AS HAPPY AS YOUR DOG?
by Alan Cohen

"You will not find Munchie at the local bar nursing a beer over lost love. He has no lost love. He loves whatever is in front of him."

A fellow at one of my workshops confessed, "For years I was so miserable that I prayed to God daily to let me wake up as happy as my dog!"

I went home and thought about it. Am I as happy as my dog? Hmmmm.

I began to observe my dog Munchie, who is happy all the time. This seven-pound fuzzball is the most joyful creature I have ever seen. He lives in a state of constant delight. Deducing that this furry creature knew something I didn't know (or at least didn't remember), I decided to study Munchie's attitude and activities in the hope that I, too, might one day wake up as happy as he is.

The key to Munchie's happiness is that he lives entirely in the here and now. He has no sense of the past or future, and he is fully present with whatever is happening. You will not find Munchie at the local bar nursing a beer over lost love. He has no lost love. He loves whatever is in front of him.

Munchie regularly shows up at the front door asking to come in and play with me. Depending on what I am doing and how muddy his feet are, sometimes I let him in. The moment I open the door, he charges in. He doesn't give me a moment to change my mind. He knows what he wants, asks for it, and seizes his opportunity the instant it is offered. Munchie is a master of Carpe Diem.

When I arrive home, Munchie greets me enthusiastically. As soon as he hears my car pull up to the garage, he drops whatever he is doing anywhere on the property, and zooms to meet me. He is so delighted to see me that he barks and cries simultaneously, wags his tail so hard that he wipes up the garage floor with his furry butt, and he pees. (Munchie taught me the meaning of the phrase, "I could hardly contain myself!") This dog lives the attitude of gratitude.

Munchie offers me the same whole-hearted greeting no matter how long I have been gone. Whether I have been away for an afternoon or a month, he gives me the full red carpet welcome. When I come home after a long time he doesn't sit on his haunches with his arms folded and soberly announce, "I think it's time we discussed your commitment to our relationship." No, he is just happy to see me, and he lets me know it.

When I am not home Munchie finds plenty of other amusements. He chases cats, sniffs dead critters, naps, and tries to mount the German shepherd next door. (He's a possibility thinker!) Munchie, as far I can tell, is an enlightened being. Perhaps, if I play my cards right, one day I will wake up as happy as him.

(Excerpted from *I Had It All the Time*, copyright 1995, by Alan Cohen)

9 ELSA: I WILL ALWAYS LOVE YOU
  By Avril Joyce

"Anyone who's an animal lover of any kind will be able to tell you how these little creatures with their all-knowing glances and their hypnotic stares can easily just reach out and grab your heart strings and just not let it go but can they tell you how they manage to do all of this without us even knowing that they are doing it? No, they cannot, for it happens over time; and once it's happened, it's too late. You are theirs for all eternity."

All puppies are adorable. They all captivate a person's heart and take it hostage, but none had ever done it to me quite like my Elsa did the first moment saw her. A cuddly little white fur ball who looked so sad in the top cage at the very back. All on her own, there she was, kind of like she had been waiting for me to come into the store—and here I was.

At first, she was very withdrawn, quiet, and nervous, but who wouldn't have been? After all, she was just six weeks old. I knew instinctively that she was the one, with her sad expression and lingering looks; and even though I had told myself and my daughter that I wanted a large breed when going into the store, I knew that that desire had been dropped by the wayside. This was the little girl I was going to pledge all of my love to, and I was already quite wrapped around her little finger.

So off we went, into the car, where she lost all of her

inhibitions and came fully to life—licking, nibbling, and instantly being my baby. I named her Elsa. When Elsa was little, she had the same look that most puppies do, with the fat little round body, and pushed-in face, all of this covered in white baby-fine long wavy hair and a bushy tail that was always on the move.

However, when the adult 'American Eskimo' dog comes into its own, it looks totally different. Over time, she became a regal long-haired dog with a fluffy ivory mane adorning her neck (like a ruffle in Victorian times) and a long plush tail that sat permanently up on her back, curled up like the letter 'C.' She had grown into her skin and was now sporting a 'snout' with a pure black nose on the end of it, which matched her ebony eyes that danced on her face. She had white whiskers, and pure white eyelashes, with two little pointed ears that most of the time stood to attention.

American Eskimo dogs are very graceful and pretty with slender legs that look like they would break in two if you blew on them, but they can run like the wind when they are so inclined. They are a very sociable dog, not yappy, but love human company, and they are loyal to the bitter end no matter what.

I had just gotten out of a bad marriage after twenty-three years and was starting all over again so she had to have a name that fit the time and circumstances. All that kept going through my mind was the movie *Born Free* and the movie's star, the lion cub Elsa. This was my Elsa and we were both being 'born free.' It suited her because she had the same mischievousness that Elsa the lion cub had. This was meant to be.

As most new members of any family know, there are adjustments. Oh boy, are there adjustments! Hiding electrical cords and shoe heels seemed to be a job that was never ending but it was no big deal. Elsa was teething and preferred these two items to chew toys and so we carried on. To describe Elsa at this tender age is almost impossible. She was just plain adorable, a little seven pound ball of pure white fur, with the blackest eyes that you could ever imagine that seemed to look way past a person's soul. And the attitude! It was something else. I felt we had known each other forever. She became one of my limbs, never straying from my side from the very beginning—always there. And everyone—family and friends—never saw us apart.

I played music an awful lot back then, and Elsa did something that absolutely floored me one night. I was playing Dolly Parton singing "I will always love you," when suddenly I heard this piercing howl, much larger than Elsa was at the time. I turned around and was just thrilled to see this little head pointed in the direction of the sky, just in full howl.

This is something that she would do right up until the time she lost her hearing at about twelve years of age, but it was really strange because she would only do it to that song, and sung only by that artist. If another artist sang the same song, she was not interested at all, nor would she howl this way if Dolly Parton sang another song. Elsa showed not the slightest twitch of interest whatsoever. Many people saw and heard this, and I was told to get her on film, but sadly it never got done. I sure regret it now because her howling was absolutely fascinating. I wish I could show you now, but wherever she is, I am sure the little 'entertainer' is doing her 'recital' on a cloud for someone else, God bless her.

It was easy to love this little angel of mine and I truly believe her to be Heaven sent. Even in those very confusing and emotional days, she understood all of my moods, my sadness, and my happy times, my ups and my downs. Never once did she give up on me—she was always there—and the love grew and grew.

Elsa and I were never apart. When she was a baby, she would sleep on my bed with me in the crook of my knees. She would just cuddle up to me there. Then as she grew in size and for the rest of her adult life, she would sleep cuddled against my back. She would lie there with her head touching the back of mine on the pillow. This I loved, as it was oh so comforting.

Towards the latter end of her life she could not jump on the bed, as she had some arthritis in her back end, so she would sleep either right under the bed, or just at my side on the carpet on the floor, but all in all, she never left my side. Sometimes I would help her onto the bed, and that was great with her too. Up my back, she would go.

When I first got her, the time coincided with the birth of my grandchildren. She hated them crying—it stressed her out—and she would look to me to fix it, with those big black eyes of hers saying, "Mummy, please help the baby, and make it alright because I don't know what to do." She was very attentive to them though, and would let me know just when they awoke or when they cried for something, or if they were in trouble of any kind. Elsa loved everybody: babies, people, other animals.

The only thing that Elsa really had a lot of trouble dealing with was change, in any way, shape, or form. I remember one day, we were out doing some shopping on the main street. We had called in at the drug store for our usual popsicle which we always had on a hot day. We shared it, and started walking. Then all of a sudden, out of the blue, she started barking and pulling and getting terribly agitated at something I was not aware of.

About twenty yards in front of us, a new pizza place had opened, and outside was a life-sized wooden cutout man, running with a pizza in hand. She must have been thinking, "Well, it shouldn't be there! It wasn't there before! So it shouldn't be there now!" Everyone was looking to see what was upsetting this little dog so much and then I realized what it was.

It happened in many other ways. If someone put a bag somewhere it shouldn't be or if I changed the furniture around, there was just no way that she handled it well. Somebody had to be to blame, and she would let you know it. Needless to say, I tried to avoid these problems, as she could be quite emphatic about it, but how do you explain this to a little girl who didn't want to know? It was simply, "It just shouldn't happen!" End of topic with her. Anyone living with a pet will tell you the 'love' goes both ways, so if it upsets them, you just don't do it, and the love carries on, as does mutual respect for each other.

As I said before, Elsa did not like change—change of any kind—so the next chapter in our lives together was going to be a tough one, or so I thought. You see, I had decided to make a move, and go live with my brother in Georgetown, Ontario. I thought that this might be extremely hard on her but to my amazement, she took to it just like a duck to water, and she absolutely loved it the whole time we were there and that happened to be about two and a half to three years.

My brother's home already was like the pages from a James Herriot book. There were already three other dogs, all of them much larger breeds than my little girl: There was Blazer, a black lab guide dog, who belonged to a friend of my brother's, and then there was my brother's own two dogs, Shadoe and Sheila, (a mother and daughter combo of Australian Cattle dogs.) All in all, with myself, my brother, my brother's friend Sam (a blind man), and the four dogs, it was a full house. But let's face it—the dogs 'ruled' and that would be an understatement.

All four dogs would pile into my brother's van every day and go to the woods with him for their exercise, and they all loved it. Elsa absolutely adored my brother. She still had her hearing at this time, so he was known to her as 'Daddy Russ.' He was another softy when it came to being wrapped around the finger. He would have more trouble with Elsa in the woods than the other three dogs put together, and he would often look to these other dogs for help with her because she would disappear on him and get into things that were actually none of her business. Her favorite pastime was to find 'dead things' and roll in them. Let's just say that my brother, more often than not, would come in the door after some of these outings before she did with an apology and a grin all over his face. Her favorite thing to do in the woods was to sort out the dead stuff and come home to mummy wearing it.

She would ultimately end up in the bath, nine nights out of ten, and she would be presentable again till the next day, but she absolutely loved it. And the love grew stronger and stronger if that were at all possible. This little girl certainly knew how to get people in the palm of her hand.

Anyone who's an animal lover of any kind will be able to tell you how these little creatures with their all-knowing glances and their hypnotic stares can easily just reach out and grab your heart strings and just not let it go, but can they tell you how they manage to do all of this without us even knowing that they are doing it? No, they cannot, for it happens over time; and once it's happened, it's too late. You are theirs for all eternity.

These animals are only 'on loan' to us for a short time, so we'd better use our time wisely, as that time can go by in a flash and quite often does. And as people who have lost pets realize, you only get that one chance, so you'd better use it every day for all that its worth. It is precious—oh so precious—and once it's gone, it is never retrievable.

Our stay with my brother Russ, Sam the blind friend, and the dogs came to an end in the latter part of 1999 when Elsa and I moved back to Mississauga to be closer to my children and grandchildren. I took an apartment, got a job, and we carried on together. There was a bit of a problem though, as Elsa didn't make this adjustment as easily as she had made the previous one.

There were periods of time when I would look at her and notice that she was aging but still adorable, and the funny part of it all was that when I developed eyesight problems, so had she; and when I began with arthritis, so did she, and what was happening seemed part of life—we were going to be two little old ladies together—and I thought that kind of cute, and it was.

Around 2004, something happened that really frightened me. Elsa went into 'heat' but something was not right. I took her to the vet as I really thought she had a prolapse of the womb. The vet told me not to worry, that she was getting older and she was swollen, but that was all. He did blood tests and checked all the other things. She ended up coming home with me that night.

But I was not satisfied. She was not in pain but she just didn't look 'right' down there. I had to go by what the vet told me and he said it was normal but I knew it wasn't. The next morning, I changed vets. When the new one did the tests again, as soon as he checked her down there, he was highly disturbed just as I had been the previous day. It definitely was not normal. It had nothing to do with her age but was a huge fibroid tumor, and it was halfway hanging outside of her.

For the first time since we had begun our journey together, we spent that night separately, as the doctor whisked her into the operating room to see what he could do. I must have called at least a dozen times in that twenty-four hour time period, and in the end, she was strong. She was otherwise tremendously healthy, and very fit for her age, so he operated.

That turned out to be one of the longest nights of my life, and I cried. Oh boy, did I cry. Elsa was able to come home the very next day, and talk about happy! I really don't know just who was the happiest—me or her—the little tail was wagging so vigorously I thought she may just wag it right off. But I know at the time, if I had a tail, then mine would have been going a mile a minute, too. There would have been quite a competition, to see just whose tail was wagging the most. I was so thrilled to see her, as she was to see me, and the tumor was all gone.

However, the one thing that the vet did tell me was that on the rare occasion these things can grow back again, but not to worry. My baby was here, she was alright, and she was home. And so our little journey kept on going, both of us side by side, loving each other. The tumor was gone, and although what the vet had said always at the back of my mind, I really tried to not think of it.

When Elsa had to have the operation, I thought I would lose her that day, and it was as close as I wanted to get to even the idea of such a thing happening, so I put it out of my mind. I suppose this was my mind's way of using a coping mechanism, and it worked. She was very happy, and seemed to be much more comfortable, which of course she was because it had been very large for how small a dog Elsa was—a mere twenty-three pounds.

She seemed to behave a lot more like she was a puppy again. She would run and play and jump, much more than before, and I noticed that she was even more tolerant of other dogs around her. She loved many things especially the 'leash free,' but with her eyesight faltering and her hearing going, it was a 'comedy of errors.' She would inevitably lose us and wander in the opposite direction, only to be chased down by myself, and whoever was with us until she realized she was quite happy but following the wrong people. I would just smile at the people, and explain that she was almost deaf and practically blind until everyone would smile.

So this was our life together. She was getting more tired these days, but that was alright, because so was I. We just put it down to age, and we both agreed that was what it was. There were a lot of times now when she would develop different funny little habits. She would come up on my knee and get as close as she could underneath my chin, more often than not burying her head there, but soon I realized she did that because she could feel the vibrations in my throat when I was speaking and she liked that. We would sit for a couple of hours or more at night time like that, and she would fall asleep to my voice, which would probably be just a 'droning' sound to her, but she found it to be very soothing and she felt connected.

Other times, she would scratch the carpet as if burying a bone or something valuable, and it was very loud, very loud indeed. That was alright with me, as she was not hurting the carpet, although sometimes I would wonder if she was headed for China, but it would happen during the night too, and it would wake anybody from a very deep sleep, it was so frantic.

I did talk to the vet about that one, and I asked him if there was anything I could do, because it would be very scary in the middle of the night. He said it was age and just to 'love her,' which I of course did, so no problem.

Her eating habits too were changing. She enjoyed everything she saw me put into my mouth, and I do mean everything, from lettuce leaves, pickled onions, celery, grapes, the whole lot. In fact the only thing she refused point blank to eat was peas. She just hated them! With peas, she was just like a child, only where a child might disguise the fact by hiding them, she would sort them out of the food and just toss them out of the dish willy-nilly. Her little idiosyncrasies reminded me of an elderly person and that is how I treated her. There were little bits of things that she didn't like, and that was fine with me. The vet had said, "Just love her," so I did. I "just loved her," weird habits and all. For the next couple of years we just plodded on with our journey. We were getting older, but we were happy.

Elsa seemed to slow down an awful lot, and sleep seemed to become one of her favorite past times, but that was no problem. Some people might say, "She's no spring chicken anymore," and we knew it, but she really loved life. Oh boy did she love life.

People told me to be quiet when I would casually mention that I did not know what I was going to do when her 'time came,' as one thing I am is a realist, and I knew soon that it would be her time to be called 'home.' She was getting feeble and actually putting on a brave face for my benefit, but I knew her too well, and I could see right through her facade.

Then, one day, it happened. A downward spiral began. I tried hard to tell myself that I was imagining it, but deep inside my heart knew I wasn't. Alright, so here it was again— Christmas time with all of its hustle and bustle just like always but Elsa had gone into 'heat,' which normally happened just prior to this season, but this year there was a difference.

For a start, she also didn't seem to be thrilled with too many people around as she normally was. At first her 'heat' was normal, and then all of a sudden, overnight, it went very heavy, far too heavy to be normal. It was so scary that I phoned the vet and made an appointment. He could see her that same hour, so we went. My daughter took us and she seemed to not be worried, but I knew something had to be very wrong—very wrong indeed.

He did all the blood tests, X-rays, and he checked everything out. Her temperature was elevated, and so he said she could possibly have an infection, and he gave us antibiotics, and sent us home. He said he wouldn't have the blood test results back until the next day so we made another appointment for the following evening.

But that night, she started to bleed even heavier, and even though on the antibiotics, she got worse. When she got up from lying down, she left blood stains all over the floor, so I put thick towels underneath her, which seemed to make her more comfortable, but she was still bleeding. Her fur was just bright red and it was very frightening. Although I tried very hard not to let Elsa see me concerned, I was truly terrified. This was not right, and it couldn't be the beginning of the end, could it? We weren't ready for this! It just couldn't be.

Now it was Friday night, and so we went to the vet again. The blood test results said that the white platelets were elevated, pointing to something wrong with the kidneys and liver. The X-rays showed no abnormality that they could see. He asked if the medication seemed to be changing anything so I told him not so far. He gave me an emergency number that I could use, in case anything happened that was unforeseen over that weekend.

We made an appointment for Monday and we went home. I did a huge amount of praying that weekend. It was terrifying and Elsa kept staring at me with those eyes that were so dimmed now, but could still look right into my very core and see my soul. I know that she knew I was completely terrified, but I was Mummy, and I knew all of the answers, didn't I? All but this one, the answer was clear: this time I couldn't make it better. It was in God's hands and He was the one calling the shots, and I believed Him to be telling us that it was time for my baby to go on home to Him. It could not have been any clearer.

I knew in my heart of hearts that we had been given these last couple of days to do and say all there was left to do or say to each other, and so we just spent that weekend loving each other.

I do not really know if animals know about death but she certainly knew that there was some sort of urgency in what was happening, and everything that she wanted to do. It didn't matter whether it was day or night, we just did it. She went outside, she walked through every puddle, she sniffed at everything that was growing, and she examined all of the things, to make sure nothing had been moved. I gave her anything she wanted and we stayed up all night—both Friday, Saturday, and Sunday—and when she slept, well then, it was my turn to sleep with her on the floor so I did.

On the Monday morning I phoned up the vet and we had a long discussion as to how she had done over the weekend. He is a wonderful man and he had seen how upset I had been but he wanted to see her because she was still bleeding and the antibiotics had not worked at all.

We went back to see him that evening when he checked her weight only to find that she had gone down from 23 pounds to just above 17, which is an enormous amount of weight for a little dog to lose. He took her into the back. I waited in the examining room for about five to ten minutes, but it felt like forever to me.

I could tell by his face when he returned, that the news was—as I had thought—inevitable. They had examined her internally as best they could, and it was a certainty that the tumor had come back. Yes, those were the words that I had never wanted to hear.

The vet went on to say that the tumor had not only returned but was further up inside her and was ulcerated, which was why she was bleeding so much. Then he carried on: Elsa had lived a good long time, and had a good life, and been loved, and even if they operated on the tumor, she would most likely not come through it because her blood work showed that her liver and kidneys were not functioning as they should be. He went on to say that the operation would be very invasive and she was obviously not a young dog anymore; being a senior, she might not recuperate properly, and this was vital.

And then he just looked at me. I held my breath. The vet told me that the kindest thing to do would be to let her go. I felt like I had been hit with a big sledge hammer.

He assured me she was not in pain so I could bring her to a different hospital the next morning at 10 o'clock. So, with my heart fragmented into a million pieces, I took Elsa my angel home. We knew it was for the last time, but it was also some sort of miracle that we were to get one more night together. I was relieved I had gotten a ride to the vet's that Monday evening from a friend. We drove home in silence so deep you could have heard a pin drop. Elsa sat on my lap with my arms were curled around her tightly.

Once in the driveway, my tears came but I somehow was able to make them silent tears. We just did the normal stuff so as not to draw attention to anything being different. I did not want her scared. I don't think either of us really slept that night. I sort of became a robot and things seemed very surreal. It did not feel like anything was wrong and yet at the same time everything was wrong. All of these feelings were so foreign and so strange.

We saw the dawn break, and somehow even though it was snowing, it seemed way too bright outside to be real. I don't really know, I guess denial was going to be there right up till the end. Oh my gosh, those words: 'the end.' They sounded not real in my head, so not real! How could this be happening? We went out to the car where two of my daughters sat waiting. Elsa stopped to go to the bathroom, and then on my lap in the car, she got settled in for our last journey together.

When we got there, the vet met us a little after ten that Tuesday morning, and he took us straight through to the back room, where I held onto Elsa with all the strength I could muster. My daughters came in with me, and there was a little conversation but not much. There was nothing more left to say. The vet took her from me, and explained what would happen. He would take her downstairs and put in the intravenous. When she came back, she would have a little blue band aid on her front leg just to hold it in place. I agreed to pass her over. She liked him, she trusted him, and she would be alright.

They then asked if I wanted to stay in the room. They bought in a chair for me to sit on while I held her; and so in she came, with her blue band aid on.

She was placed on my lap once more. Both of my daughters kissed her and said their 'goodbyes.' Then there was just myself, my darling little girl Elsa, and the vet.

I really do not think I could have held onto her any tighter as the needle went in. I talked and talked and talked to her as comfortingly as I knew how, and I did not break down. All of a sudden, all too quickly, she fell asleep, and in doing so, her head fell and rested right on top of my heart. I am sure she could feel it beating.

I kept hugging and talking, and then she was gone. The vet said that she was at peace and that I could put her down but I could not put her down just yet. I repeated to her that it was alright to go home. Mummy would be alright, and I told her that I would always love her, and that I would never stop.

I laid her on a blue towel on the table that the vet had put down for me but I was still holding onto her, cradling her head and talking in her ear. By this time I could hardly see through my tears, as they now were coming fast and furious. He was trying to console me, but to no avail. My heart was completely broken, and it was then that he asked my daughters to come back into the room again.

I took some scissors out of my purse and cut some of her beautiful white fur from her. He gave me an envelope to put it in, and I thanked him. I also took her collar and put it in my purse. I really don't remember leaving the hospital, don't remember much at all of anything, except my daughters telling me that they had paid to get her ashes. I could not have done this myself and it surprised me, but at the same time, made me feel so wonderful to know that my children had done this last thing for me because I could not have afforded it myself.

I went home, even though my girls wanted me to go home with one of them. Somehow, I needed to go home. I looked around at things: at the dog dishes, with food still in them, and two towels still on the floor, where she had been lying. I decided to just leave them there, so I did. I felt very odd, as though someone had taken a couple of my limbs away and pulled my heart right from my chest. For the next two weeks, my house was unbearably quiet and strange. My heart was in disrepair, but it also felt very serene and still which I had a hard time dealing with.

I had many phone calls, most of which I did not answer, as I did not want to keep talking about what had happened. I was not trying to be rude. It was just that this was my way of coping. I went inside myself, with my thoughts, and memories. I could deal with that. It was safe there.

After two weeks, I got the phone call to come and pick up her ashes, and a friend went for me to do this, and when he came in with this tiny urn. I cried and cried, so much that I thought it would never end. My baby was finally where she belonged. She was with me; she had come home. With any death there is a grieving process that the person or persons left behind have got to go through. This is inevitable. And I was no exception to this rule, but the one thing that I had trouble with, was my feelings of guilt. I found it hard to swallow that it was me who put pen to paper and signed her name—and even though I knew then as I know now that this was the right thing to do—the guilt was so overwhelming. Her tiny white urn coming home to where she belonged helped somewhat, but still I was so shattered. The biggest turning point seemed to be the day that I spoke with my brother Russ, because something very mysterious had happened to me on the previous night, and as I was telling him about it, he told me something that completely changed my mind.

He told me of a lady had just had on his radio show, whom he had spoken to about his dogs that had died a couple of years earlier. He asked me if I'd email her, because she had truly helped him make peace with it all, so I decided to do it. What could happen so I sent the letter. It went like this,

"Hi there,

My brother, Russ Horton, was actually blown away with what you had told him. We run a web site together, and animals are a big part of it. Up until recently, I had a little dog, whose name was Elsa. She was my baby. I had her for almost 16 years, and lost her to sickness that was very sudden, on January 21, at 10:32 a. m. and I seem to be feeling weird things. Something happened a week ago, and I was wondering if you could shed some light on this for me...I would be very obliged."

I went on to write: "I'd been waiting for a sign from my Elsa, and just last night, during the night, I awoke to a very overpowering feeling of what I can only describe as peace. I could feel her. She was actually all around, and it was actually all encompassing. I could not see Elsa, but I felt an overwhelming feeling that things where as they should be. This had not happened before that night. It was such an overly powerful feeling, that I got up so that I could check things out. Obviously, there was nothing there to see, but I know what I felt and I could really feel her.

I stayed up for some time, as the feeling was so warm and comforting. I did not want to go back to bed and take the risk of losing it. It was similar to the feeling that a parent gets when their child eventually comes home from being out, and you realize that they are safe, and where they should be.

After a while, I did go back to bed of course and when I lay down, I heard her BREATHING. I jumped up to find where this sound was coming from and it was coming from nowhere. It was everywhere. Elsa had a very distinctive sound when breathing. She wheezed like a little old man, and it was definitely her breathing. I realized that I was not imagining any of this! I said to myself, "I'm wide awake, I am not a crazy lady, and I do think rationally most of the time. This is truly happening!"

After a while I returned to bed, feeling very peaceful, and relaxed, and went to sleep to the comforting sound of my precious baby breathing. The feeling was not there when I woke up, but I didn't care, because I knew what I felt in the night, and it was real. All I can say is, it was a comforting and very happy presence. If it happens again, I would welcome the experience because it was awesome.

My answer came to me the very next day when Amelia wrote back.

"Hi Avril. I want to tell you how beautiful I think this letter is, and yes, when I was on your brother's radio show, I did "look" and see the two "angel" dogs in your brother's bed. One was his own and the other was the spirit of a little white fluffy dog who had come to visit. Your brother told me you had heard this little white angel dog breathing in your bed.

You are not a crazy lady. The love of my life, Aunt Flo, was my kitty who died last February. She has been able to shake the bed in five different hotel rooms and stomp up my body, waking me out of a dead sleep. Your Elsa is really there.

My next book is about animals who communicate messages from heaven. I'd be honored if you let me publish your story. Would you be willing to share Elsa with the world? She could melt a thousand hearts."

This is the message I had been waiting for. You can guess how I felt. This definitely was the turning point, and she had told me what I wanted to hear and really did know was true. My Angel baby was indeed truly with me.

I was so thrilled to have this confirmed that my answer back to Amelia was a resounding "YES, YES!" I was positive about the fact that my little girl would be able to melt a thousand hearts as she had in her lifetime. She would certainly be able to do this in death.

I now accept that she is here with me. No, I cannot see her physical body but I feel her around all of the time. Her absence would be a more obvious feeling to me, but I do not get that feeling. I get a very serene, peaceful, and all-encompassing love, which is the opposite of what I would be experiencing if she were not here.

What happened that first night—when I heard her breathing—has happened twice since then, and each time I look for the source, but I never find it. I guess I am not meant to but that is alright because it leaves me with the knowledge that wherever she may be, the best part of her is still here, with her mummy.

When a beloved pet passes, their love, their energy, and their very being has got to live on. Where else would it go? These loved ones do not die. It is not possible for 'energy' to die for it is just the physical body that passes away, not the soul.

So, in conclusion, I would just like to add, that I am honored to have shared my little Angel Elsa with everyone, and please remember, that wherever there is love, it will always be--for love does not die. So the love that she had inside of her little heart and soul for everyone, including myself, is still here. So we go forward, loving each other just as much as in life, but in a slightly different way, and I thank God for that, for that means it will be forever, and nobody can take 'forever' away. God bless the animals.

Now, I have to tell you something very mysterious. On my board, we try to get orphaned animals homed, and there I saw this senior cat called T.C. come up last November. Try as I did, I could not find this poor creature a home. It was already 6 years old and was supposedly nasty with other cats, so she really did not sound like she had a lot going for her. I felt so bad at the time, as the people who had her were kicking her and keeping her down a small dark, unfinished basement. She never saw the light or had human contact, and she never got any interaction of any kind.

I would have taken her just to get her out of that situation, but with Elsa in her twilight years, I thought it would be unfair to her. However, this cat came up on the board again about 5 months ago and she was still living under these same situations. I tried to go to sleep one night and try as I might, this cat was on my mind. It was a very strange being 'nagged' by someone. Anyway, the urging went on all night and finally I gave in and told myself that it was what I was supposed to do. I felt like permission had been given but the nagging in my head was really incredible.

So, although it was not in my plans, I now have "Little Biddy," and this cat lies in Elsa's favorite spots only and comes on the bed at night. Although I never thought I would have a cat, now I do, but

I really don't think it was my idea. And although she is beautiful I had never really been a cat person, always a dog person. But I think Elsa told me to go get her. What do you think?

10 KALI: WHISPER OF A KISS
By Marie Mead

"I would find myself with thoughts I had never entertained before—like the fact that there are millions of non-humans on this planet, each with his or her unique personality, and I knew only a few of them intimately. Sometimes I found myself wishing I could live millions of years in this lifetime just so I could experience the wonder of the world's many creatures. My fantasies would come to an end when the black-skirted bunny flounced into view. I had been given an opportunity to know this rabbit, and I wasn't going to daydream away that opportunity."

"...wants a rabbit?"

"Do you know anyone who wants a rabbit?"

My friend Judy, who had just begun working at a preschool, posed the simple question.

I shook my head. But strangely, my hand, seemingly of its own volition, rose into the air.

My inner critic reacted: What are you doing? You don't know anything about rabbits. You don't have time. Tell her NO!

Something stopped me from voicing those thoughts. Instead, my heart listened to Judy: the rabbit, confined to a small wire cage, endured frequent jabs as children tried to get him to "do something." His lunging at a child's finger prompted the search for a new home.

My ignorance and my arrogance appeared hand in hand. How hard can a rabbit be? You already know a lot about animals—you can learn as you go. With those thoughts, I got ready to prepare for my first rabbit.

The next day was a whirlwind of activity. I obtained a referral to a veterinarian experienced in treating rabbits. Sandwiched into a hectic work schedule, I purchased food, checked out library books, and called rescue organizations for additional information.

Within twenty-four hours the doorbell rang, announcing the arrival of the alleged "healthy, six-month-old male bunny." I opened the door, little knowing that I was about to open my heart—wide.

Eagerly, I peered into the small, dilapidated wire cage. Expecting bright eyes and a lively little bunny, I instead saw dark, vacant eyes in a body that seemed devoid of life. My heart sank. This was not what I had anticipated. Something was dreadfully wrong.

The next morning's visit to the vet clinic revealed shocking news: "he" was a two-and-a-half-year-old female bunny, so malnourished and ill from mistreatment and neglect that she was dying.

"She might live a week," the vet said.

I was shocked. My first bunny ... and she wasn't going to live more than a week? I just could not accept that outcome for this beautiful little creature.

Having been involved with animal rescue for years, I had seen seriously abused and neglected animals rebound before, and I was not about to give up on this rabbit. Within seconds, I transformed from concerned animal-lover into a student of emergency medical treatment. Appropriate measures were taken at the clinic. Then, under the vet's expert guidance, my first rabbit—who I had envisioned happily hopping about the house—became my at-home patient.

Oh, how she distrusted humans. When it came to taking medication, Kali (as I named her) would kick and struggle, twist and turn. She was small and fragile in body only—the rest of her was a mix of spunk and determination. It didn't help that I was timid and uncertain when I had to hold her. I had read enough to know that a rabbit's musculoskeletal system is delicate, and so I was afraid of inadvertently causing harm.

A week passed, then another. That she lived was a miracle. That her three-pound body contained seemingly unlimited iron will was a revelation. That she changed my life was other-worldly.

One of the first things I needed to do was earn her trust, so I began spending time at her eye level. After two-and-a-half years in the classroom, she needed someone who showed interest without forcing interaction and contact. I would lie on the floor, papers around me, pausing frequently in my work to watch this new family member. She would examine me from a short distance away, her nose seeming to twitch a hundred times a minute as she assessed who I was.

"You are so beautiful," I would whisper.

And oh, she was. Kali was an American fuzzy lop, with eyes the color of fine dark chocolate. Her eyelids were heavily fringed by short hairs, with several long black whiskers above her eyes making it look as though she had gorgeous, impossibly long eyelashes. Lop ears draped to perfectly frame her sweet face. Kali's three-and-a-half pound body was fine-boned and delicate, covered in silky black fur that hung down to the floor, hiding her feet. The fur parted over her spine, as though someone had taken a comb and meticulously divided the hair down the middle of her back.

But then she moved, and I cringed at the crackling sound emanating from her. It was arthritis, the vet had advised, resulting from extended living in the too-small wire cage.

She tried to hop. I cried. She ended up spread-eagle on the floor. I knew there was nothing the vet could do to compensate for Kali's early years of confinement in that cage, with the wire floor cutting into her tender feet. In addition to chronic discomfort caused by the arthritis, Kali had misshapen feet, broken toes, undeveloped leg muscles, and severely splayed front legs. Useful only to help steer about, the forelegs could not bear any weight; they would slide back against her sides when she was at rest. One of her back legs was obviously weak, causing her to tilt slightly when sitting.

There was more. Gastrointestinal and bladder problems, wayward third eyelids, probable neuromuscular damage, anemia… Over time, I came to realize that she was also deaf. In human terminology, Kali had multiple, permanent disabilities.

Kali, however, seemed blithely unaware of any physical challenges. Her dynamic spirit forged ahead wherever she attempted to go, and everyone, including the family cats, respected her. One of them, a calico named Pepita, was as mesmerized by our beautiful rabbit as I was. And so it was that Kali gained a cat guardian.

One day Kali flopped over on her side and lay still against a wall. "NO!" The word lodged in my throat. Oh God, don't take her from me, I silently begged.

Pepita had already run to Kali and was nudging her face … and my intrepid rabbit came back to life. I laughed with joy as she indignantly moved to a more hidden resting spot. Although I never again felt my heart in my throat when Kali did a bunny flop, I must admit to checking to make sure she was still breathing.

As Kali incrementally regained health, I found creative ways to provide care. I was fortunate to have rabbit-knowledgeable people offer assistance. One of them, an occupational therapist, showed me simple exercises that helped strengthen Kali's muscles and some inventive ways to help keep her dry, so important because her tissue-thin skin was susceptible to urine burn.

I developed a system of hand signals for my little deaf darling, though I still talked to her as was my habit. She quickly learned the signal for her favorite leafy greens. She knew the sign for her play room and would race ahead of me to get there. Kali didn't react quite as nicely, though, when I would give the hand signal to pick her up. She would grunt and sometimes charge with wide-open mouth! As much as I knew she hated being handled, I would not give her that choice—her long fur needed grooming, and she also benefitted from hands-on therapy.

How blessed I was to have her in my life. Caring for her was service work unlike anything I had ever done, though she could be irascible about accepting my ministrations. But caring for her was a transformative experience, and I performed each task willingly and gratefully.

I was in awe of her. Kali offered a glimpse into the mysterious, magical world of rabbits, and every day brought a new discovery. Sometimes I would find myself talking to her about it.

"You are so incredible! What else will I learn about you?"

I would find myself with thoughts I had never entertained before—like the fact that there are millions of non-humans on this planet, each with his or her unique personality, and I knew only a few of them intimately. Sometimes I found myself wishing I could live millions of years in this lifetime just so I could experience the wonder of the world's many creatures. My fantasies would come to an end when the black-skirted bunny flounced into view. I had been given an opportunity to know this rabbit, and I wasn't going to daydream away that opportunity.

"Kali, you are so gorgeous," I would tell her time and again.

I knew she could not hear me, but it seemed she could read my mind. She would tilt her head just slightly, as if to say "I know," and then bound off to her favorite resting spot in the corner of the living room. I continued to work in the room just to be close to her. The cats usually joined me, and together we would watch our newest family member.

Sometimes she would come over to investigate what I was doing, shuffling my papers with her ungainly movements. I loved it when she showed enough trust to give me a friendly bump on my arm. She liked gentle strokes on the inside of her long ears and rubs around their base; I would pet her face and massage her jaws. Sometimes she'd rapidly move her mouth, making a contented "purring" sound. Kali was a whole new experience.

She was a feisty little thing, biting or nipping whenever she was displeased with what I was doing. But Kali instinctively lived the adage, "Don't bite the hand that feeds you." I found it highly amusing that she never went after my fingers. Strange though it may sound, I was happy to be on the receiving end of Kali's teeth. As long as she was fighting for her right to be free, I was certain she would be able to overcome the difficulties brought on by her early mistreatment.

Kali was strong in other likes and dislikes: She loved curly-leaf kale but hated mustard greens, displayed obvious delight when eating fresh-picked oregano or dill, but snubbed the herbs if purchased from the store. She wanted to be fed no later than 6:00 a.m.—if I was a minute late, she would start thumping, then pick up her heavy food bowl and bang it on the floor. Her evening routine was a little different: she would give me a baleful stare and pull on my shoestrings if I happened to walk past empty-handed at feeding time. I tried to refrain from laughing, to no avail.

"You are perfect, Kali," I assured her.

I hoped my father would think the same; he was coming for a week-long visit. Having grown up in a household devoid of animals—as was common for his time and place—he saw an animal's rightful place as being outside. So when he saw Kali's house and playpen in the living room, with stray pieces of grass hay scattered about the floor, I wondered what his reaction would be.

Dad walked over, looking down at the small being who was browsing on hay. He had a look of puzzlement on his face, as though not quite sure how to react. I don't think he planned to pet her, but all of a sudden he knelt down and reached out to stroke Kali's head.

She reacted to this stranger's presence immediately, slicing his finger. My father silently rocked back on his heels.

Then, with a sheepish grin, he said, "Well, I guess I know just what she thinks of me."

And that was the start of Dad's one-sided love affair with a rabbit. After he returned home, our daily conversations always started with the same question: "How is that little black rabbit today?" Sometimes he didn't remember her name, but that didn't matter because it was her spirit that had captured him, as it had captured me.

My father felt a bond with Kali for other reasons. Like her, he was deaf, had been seriously mistreated, and now was in a phase of life where he needed some care from others. Both my father and I were humbled by Kali's attitude toward life. She was our inspiration.

Dad and I had a close—though difficult—relationship, and Kali became our bridge to communicating more openly and freely. Due to caring for a disabled rabbit, I was able to better care for my father. I found myself thinking more creatively in meeting his needs, providing daily challenges to make his life more interesting and to keep him independent for as long as possible. Kali was the reason for the changes in me, and I frequently gave thanks for her presence in my life. For brief moments, I understood the meaning of selfless love, and those periods of time were glorious.

Kali regained enough health that the vet thought it safe to spay her. Though I was concerned about the surgery, I also knew that after spaying she would benefit from a furred companion. Indeed, that is what happened. Once recovered, she was paired with a gentle bunny named Kumar (meaning "prince"), who lived up to his name and became Kali's comfort and protector.

They were a sweet-looking couple. Kumar's short white fur contrasted beautifully with Kali's silky black covering. His expressive pink eyes alerted me to his anxieties and fears, while her dark fathomless eyes continued to bar me from knowing her secrets.

It was Kumar who showed me how acrobatic rabbits can be as he performed a frolic in space. When he was sure that his mate was safe and well, he'd race around the room, then leap and twist in mid-air. I wished Kali was able to perform such normal rabbit feats, but Kumar seemed to understand that the task was his and so he entertained us with his antics.

I became enamored of Kumar, loving the way he cared for Kali. He would groom her and offer his body as a bolster when she grew tired. Knowing she was deaf, he would thump loud resonating warnings that she sensed through her feet. Kumar was perfect, offering me yet another glimpse into the incredible world of rabbits.

One day when visiting a friend, I watched as one of her bunnies ran up to bestow kisses on my friend's arm. The closest thing I had to knowing what that felt like was her explanation: warm, soft, barely damp tongue that was smooth, not raspy like a cat's tongue. I wanted to get one of those kisses from Kali. I knew she trusted me, but receiving a kiss would, I decided, be the ultimate gift from her.

Upon my return home, I visualized and communicated my desire to Kali. Nothing happened. I coaxed and begged. I even crushed a papaya tablet—a favorite treat—and sprinkled some of it on my arm. No deal. I wasn't really surprised. By this time I knew that Kali's life was going to be lived on her terms.

Through all this, Kali had good days and bad days. Since rabbits cannot tolerate pain well, I watched for the subtle signs of discomfort. In addition to her proclivity toward respiratory illness, Kali's digestive system was easily disrupted. I was mindful of gastrointestinal stasis, a silent painful killer of rabbits, and one day it suddenly happened. Kali became ill with an upper respiratory infection, her system slowed down, and then she went into stasis. For days I nursed her, having learned how to administer subcutaneous fluids, maintain her body temperature, and give pain medication. Syringe feedings were necessary too, though I generally wore more of the food than she ingested. For such a small fragile being, she was a handful!

To me, Kali was a paradox: soft, fuzzy, and small in

stature (tiny, really), but chock full of mutinous, rebellious, willful—albeit charming—personality. It wasn't that I expected a sweet cuddly being in the form of a rabbit, but she was just such a total surprise. I never expected a rabbit to be so hell-bent on getting her own way. Kali had unlimited capacity for expressing who she was, and she celebrated life with bravery, impertinence, and vitality.

Then came the downturn, nearly four years after coming to live with me. It started slowly, without any signs of illness or injury. It had been inevitable that her life would be shortened due to her early experiences at the preschool. But I had hoped she would live a normal lifespan, giving me more time with her.

But she had already lived longer than expected. I knew that love, attentive care, and Kumar's companionship had helped Kali maintain her zest for life. But I knew there was something more: a Higher Power was at work. I didn't think it was coincidence that four years earlier my arm had been pulled into the air, saying yes to this particular rabbit. Now it was becoming time to let her go. I wasn't ready for that. Veterinary check-ups, performed at home, became part of our regular routine. Then one day Kali lacked spirit and seemed unusually tired. As I tended her, she was strangely docile. She didn't nip when I picked her up; instead, she lay quietly against me.

"Is it time for you to leave us, Kali?"

She didn't stir.

"I want you to give me a sign, Kali. If you want me to help you transition, give me a sign."

And I did not want just any sign. I wanted Kali to give me a kiss.

Nothing, not a whisper of movement. She remained unnaturally still against my shoulder, seemingly uninterested in life. Kumar jumped onto the footstool and stepped onto my lap to be close to his ladylove. He had a worried expression in his pink eyes.

I set her gently on the floor. Kumar immediately

bolstered her fragile body. After about an hour, Kali had enough energy to hop to the condo and eat. The next morning, she was again her lively little self. I was relieved; so was Kumar. But hours later, she took another downturn. She ate a little, but I couldn't take heart from that action alone because rabbits will often eat to hide their vulnerability.

Kali again acted in ways uncharacteristic to her; she objected to nothing, not even being held. She did not want to move, and it seemed as though her one good leg had lost its strength. Because of the chronic discomfort from arthritis, the vet had prescribed pain medication, but what I was seeing could not be attributed to pain. Given her history and physiological condition, I knew that if this current state continued, Kali would suffer—and that was something I could prevent.

I called the vet's office, and he admitted that he thought her time had come, that she was not going to recover this time. I hated hearing him say it. Dejected, I sat on the floor, watching Kumar groom his beloved sweetheart. There was no sign of her previous unflagging spirit. I made the arrangements for the vet to come the next morning, his final visit to see Kali.

I wouldn't cry. She was still alive and I wanted to immerse myself in her presence, cherishing each remaining moment. I spent hours that night gazing at Kali—wishing her life would go on and on—wishing I had more time with her. But I was filled with gratitude that I had the chance to know her at all.

It was obvious the next morning that I had made the right decision. But still I questioned myself. It had not been easy to choose the option of ending her precious life, though it seemed the kindest thing to do.

It was nearly time. I picked Kali up and sat in our chair; Kumar joined us. The front door opened; I tensed. Kumar looked at me for assurance—but I couldn't give him any.

I questioned the vet. "Isn't there anything else we can do for her? Is there something we could have missed?"

He understood what I was asking, but could only shake his head and offer his sympathy. He waited in silence. I could not say the words. I just looked at him, beseeching him to help me—to help her.

Kali never moved, not even when the needle administered the sedative. Her small body relaxed. The vet looked at me, letting me know that the second injection would make it final. Did I want to change my mind? I wanted to. Oh, I wanted to with all my heart.

"I have to let her go."

The words caught like burrs in my swollen throat. I watched with horror as the dose was administered—wanting to scream at him to stop.

"Kali," I yelled her name silently. "KALI!"

Her body became lighter. Our Kali was gone. I held onto her, wanting to capture her warmth. I rearranged silky fur, thinking how odd it was that I could groom her and not cause discomfort. She was gone, but I could not seem to get my thoughts around what that meant.

Tears flowed down my face and fell onto her body. I did not want her to get mussed, so I wiped my face, willing myself not to cry. Kumar was looking at me, wanting Kali with him. I jolted back into responsibility. How could I have forgotten Kumar?

I laid her body on the floor, and he immediately jumped from the stool and hopped to her. He groomed her face, then the rest of her body, and then started the process over again. He nudged her, as if trying to awaken her from sleep. He groomed her some more. At times, he would look up at me, as if pleading for me to do something.

"Oh sweet Kali, come back," I heard myself say. "Please come back."

I felt weirdly adrift. It looked as though Kali was simply lying on her side in a contented bunny flop, as she had often done, and part of me kept expecting her to wake up.

After nearly two hours, Kumar gave up and lay down beside Kali's body, stretching his length alongside hers as though to keep her warm as he had always done. His body was between her and the doorway, protecting her from harm, as was his custom. His open eyes were dull and unseeing. I wished I could ease his pain.

When he finally moved away, it was with slow movements. He stopped, turned around and looked at her for a long time, and then he hopped back to her body again. One nudge, then another. At last, he moved away, this time for good. He watched as I picked her up and cradled her in my arms. Kumar did not approach again. He lay down with his head on the floor, unmoving, staring into eternity.

"I'm so sorry, Kumar. I'm so sorry, but she just couldn't go on anymore."

I wanted him to understand, and on some level I am sure he did. Kali was free of pain and discomfort, in a place where she was unfettered by her physical handicaps and could move like the acrobat she had always been, deep inside.

I wasn't sure what to do next. I didn't want to remove her body—making her death even more final—though I knew I had to. But each time I touched her, it was with the intention of loving her and holding on to her, not letting her go. I procrastinated, turning instead to the grieving Kumar.

I had a responsibility to him. Without their companion, some rabbits die of grief. Much as I did not want to put him with another rabbit—for it was always "Kali and Kumar" in my mind—I knew that being with another bunny might be the best thing for him.

Siobhan, an English spot rescued from a high-altitude meadow, had come to live with us months earlier, but she and Kali were rivals when it came to Kumar's attention. Now it was Siobhan's turn to comfort Kumar, and comfort him she did. The majestic black-and-white rabbit gently licked his face, and Kumar allowed her ministrations. Though I was thankful he would not be alone, I was not ready for Kali to be replaced. I made the decision to cremate her body so that when he died, I could spread their ashes together, symbolically reuniting them.

The day turned into a nightmare. I received two calls that threw me further into turmoil. A very special aunt had died; she had been like a second mother to me and a strong tie to my now-deceased father. The second call was to inform me that a close family member, six hours away in another city, had been admitted for emergency abdominal surgery.

Even today I have a hard time remembering those hours. Everything was surreal. My thoughts mirrored my movements: jerky. I couldn't seem to get my limbs to work. I couldn't seem to grasp the fact that Kali was gone. Kali.

The next two weeks were so chaotic that it felt as though time was suspended. I was a full participant in life at times, a fringe participant other times.

Through it all, Kali was at the back of my mind. Few people understood what she meant to me—to many, she was just a rabbit. No one had an inkling of the enormity of her presence or what she gave to me. At odd times I would think of something she did and a joyful lift would inhabit my heart. She had been so smart and sometimes so mutinous, and I would find myself smiling and shaking my head, still amazed that such a huge personality had inhabited such a fragile body.

It was those sweet memories that helped me through those weeks. I would envision Kali bouncing down the hallway, ears flopping in rhythm, and marvel at how fast she could move on only two legs. Or I would remember how she draped herself over Kumar's neck; he was always so patient, remaining still until she was ready to get up again. Sometimes I would go out at dusk, thinking like a prey animal, mindful of shadows and unfamiliar noises and scents. That was another thing for which I was grateful to her. Before Kali, I had no idea of what it meant to be a prey animal. Because of her and Kumar, I had learned about the prey psyche and now was far more compassionate than before and certainly more attuned to nature.

The days ran together; weeks passed, filled with the mundane. I functioned on automatic because I had done it so long and so often in the past weeks. My pain was tucked away somewhere. I could sense its presence but not really feel it. I was out of touch.

Some months later I was home alone, lying on the bed in a stupor. I desperately wanted to see Kali again. It was nearly dawn when I finally dozed off. Just as quickly, I startled awake.

"Kali?"

Swinging my legs out of bed, I prepared to go see if she was okay. And then I remembered and slumped back onto the bed. I felt frozen inside.

The next night, I dreamt. My father appeared.

"How's that little black rabbit?"

I smiled when I heard that familiar question, the same one he had asked during our daily phone calls. But didn't he know? He was on the Other Side, just as she was. Why did he have to ask me? I did not want to say the words. He kept looking at me, waiting for a reply.

"She's gone," I finally said.

I couldn't bring myself to use the word "dead" or "passed on." A quizzical look came over his face. Seeing that familiar look, I had to smile. I knew exactly what he was going to say.

"What makes you say that?"

The smile spread to my solar plexus. It was his favorite question, one I had heard at least a thousand times.

"She died." There, I had said it.

His look was gentle. "Rest. You need to rest."

I saw myself fall into a deep sleep. My father's presence had been comforting. I missed him and was glad to see him again. When I awoke, it was still dark and cold. I reached out for my cat, Pepita, the one who always seems to know exactly how I feel and who also had watched over Kali. She nuzzled my hand, snuggling closer for warmth.

I drifted back to sleep, to my dream. I was searching, looking above the clouds for Kali. She used to visit me in my dreams when she was alive, taking me on forays to the heavens to show me how she could run and leap and hop. I could not find her this time and felt such desolation.

My father appeared. In his arms was Kali. I wept with relief. She was safe with him. At least I knew she was sheltered in love, not somewhere "between realms," as I often thought of it. She sprang from his arms and bounded to me, as though glad to see me. I knelt down, opening my arms to receive her. She leaped, landing easily and safely in them.

"Oh, Kali, I love you. I love you so much."

She lifted her small head, her dark eyes looking into mine. I wanted to hear her say, "I love you too." But nothing came.

I laughed, "It always has to be on your terms, doesn't it?" That was Kali's way, the way it always had been.

"I'm in awe of you," I told her. "And I'll always love you."

Her body felt warm and soft. Her long silky hair brushed against my arms. Oh, she was so beautiful, so perfect.

"I miss you, Kali," I whispered. "I really miss you. So does Kumar."

At the sound of her beloved's name, she stirred and looked at me again.

"I am still with you both," I heard her say.

She started to raise herself up, as though to rest on my shoulder. It was how I loved holding her after a grooming session. I felt her nose bump my collarbone. Was she going to nip me? I would not have been surprised.

She relaxed. I thought I felt her sigh. Peace filled me. This is what I craved, holding her in serenity and love. This is how I wanted to remember her.

"I love you," I whispered softly.

She turned her head and nuzzled my neck. Such a sweet feeling.

"I'll always love you—you're embedded in my heart and soul," I said.

I could feel tears of joy welling up in me. She was fine now, in this place. She was with my father, and they were enveloped in peace and love. They always would be. When I wanted to see her, I could visit her in my dreams. And someday we would all be together.

"I love you, Kali," I said again.

Then I felt it, just a whisper of touch. Her tongue—soft, warm, licking my neck. Long awaited: Kali's kiss.

Marie Mead is the co-author of *Rabbits: Gentle Hearts, Valiant Spirits – Inspirational Stories of Rescue, Triumph, and Joy.*

11 UKIE: ON THE WINGS OF LOVE
by Brandie Kellett

"There's nothing like the feeling of meeting a mistreated animal who thinks the world is a place in which to be angry, fearful and alone and then to be able to show this wonderful soul that the world does indeed hold love. Nothing in my life has given me more satisfaction than this kind of experience with an animal—watching them discover joy and comfort for the first time. Maybe because in seeing their plight I have also seen my own and just like them, I longed to have a place to belong and to know that love was there."

The year was 1981. I was a very young lady just recently out on my own in the world. My parents had divorced six years before in a somewhat haphazard manner that hadn't included much thought of what their adolescent daughter should do with her life. I hadn't done well in school and had no skills for a career. Barely 18 and not interested in college, I worked at a coffee shop in San Diego where I had moved from New York with my father a few years before. I didn't have a car or know how to drive so I rode my bike back and forth to work. This is what filled my days back then. I had a lot of time on my hands to wonder what I would do with my life, and not a whole lot of aspirations.

In California, especially the southern part, most apartment buildings have courtyards. The building where I rented a small one bedroom apartment was no exception.

Shaped like a U, it had a courtyard in the middle decorated with a few benches and a couple of fruit trees which created somewhat of a small community area where tenants could sit, visit or barbeque.

This particular day I was just coming in from work. It was late afternoon and an unusual southern California summer rain was falling. It was then, as I climbed off my bike and walked across the courtyard toward my apartment that I saw a small cage situated on one of the benches. Sitting quietly inside was a beautiful yellow bird, about 7 inches tall with big round orange cheeks and a fancy feathered plume on the top of its head. There wasn't much room in the cage, only enough space to jump from one of two perches and back to the other, and certainly no place to take cover from the rain drops. My curiosity was immediately peaked.

Having been an animal lover all my life I had always found it somewhat irresistible when I sensed one in need or in danger. I hesitated a moment, not knowing what I should do and then went inside my apartment. It wasn't raining hard and it wasn't cold but I knew to be left out in the rain couldn't be good for the bird. I also noticed that the cage sat in front of my neighbor Jim's apartment who to my knowledge did not own a bird. He wasn't home, so I waited. Upon his arrival a short time later I immediately approached him.

"Oh, that!" he said to me as he rolled his eyes. "It belonged to my parents. It's an impossible and obnoxious thing. My father asked me to take it because he's fed up, so now I'm stuck with this bird." I considered myself pretty good with animals, especially difficult cases, so I asked him if I could try to work with it for a couple of weeks. He readily agreed, adding a sarcastic "good luck!"

So I brought this beautiful bird home. As I carried it to my apartment that first day, strange sounds started to emanate from the cage and I realized that I was being properly delivered a long hissing and squawking spell from my new friend.

She was a female Albino Cockatiel, as I would later find out. Although at the time and for at least a few years after, I thought she was a male. Then one day I arrived home to find her sitting at the bottom of her cage—on an egg. When I called the vet they told me that at a certain point birds have to use the material they carry with them to make eggs as they grow older and so "he" became a "she" and laid four tiny eggs altogether.

But on the day I found her, I took her inside and I set her cage down on my kitchen table to say hello and have a look only to be met with another long barrage of what must have been Cockatiel curses along with a peculiar battle stance where she became almost horizontal with all feathers flat against her body and her head jutted forward towards me with her beak gapping wide open. She was seven feathery inches of fury, looking as if she were about to catapult off a ski jump. It sounded like she was sneezing, squeaking and coughing all at once and at first I thought she might have indeed caught a cold from sitting outside too long. But these sounds would become all too familiar to me as the days wore on.

I learned that there wasn't much this little bird was afraid of, except hands. It didn't matter a bit that I was a hundred times her size and that she was small and caged—anything or anyone that bothered or displeased her would know about it.

The name she had been given was Ukie. I didn't know where that was from but later attended a bird show at the San Diego Wild Animal Park and discovered that they had a white and yellow Cockatoo which looked surprisingly like Ukie, just larger. The bird had the same name and could sing, "I Left My Heart In San Francisco." I could only imagine that my neighbor's family had attended the show and thought having a bird like that would be fun. Without knowing how to care for such an animal or that not all birds can talk, they had purchased Ukie with some high expectations—expectations which she had failed to meet. Many people don't understand that dogs, birds, horses and all other animals don't come ready made for life with humans. They have a different set of behaviors that are perfectly normal for them that we as humans need to acclimate ourselves to, not the other way around. Like any animal, and maybe a little more so, birds require a certain amount of patience and sensitivity. Since I soon learned that Ukie was terrified of fingers and hands, I believe she must have been grabbed and poked often in those early years, especially since she never fully recovered from this particular fear for the rest of her long life.

Understanding the signs of abuse when I saw it, I suddenly realized that maybe two weeks wasn't long enough to befriend this wild fowl after all. But fortunately I had lots of spare time. So there we sat together at our first meeting, me with my hands out of site gently telling her how beautiful she was and Ukie glaring at me between the bars of her cage, telling me where I could go.

As the days passed, I would come home from work and sit close to her cage, talking softly for long stretches of time. Slowly I started to see signs that the ice was melting. With cats, they might purr and blink their eyes. With a dog, they lower their heads and wag their tails. With Ukie I learned she would fluff up and that radiant yellow/orange plume on the top of her head would start to raise or lower depending on how she felt about what I was saying. All the while that I would speak, her dark round eyes would watch me intently.

Eventually we started having these little chats while I rested my hands in front of the cage. This took a while since every time she saw fingers, there would be a tirade of sputtering and squawking and I'd have to wait for her to calm down again. Progress was slow.

After some time, I learned that if I opened the cage door and leaned in so that my shoulder was close, she would hop on. Then we would walk around the apartment or sit on the couch. If I approached something strange while Ukie was on my shoulder, she would assume her alarm stance and shift all her weight in the opposite direction while becoming very skinny and tall. She would pull all her feathers in and turn

145

her head to the side so she could examine whatever it was with one of her very round eyes. But invariably her curiosity would get the better of her, and I became amazed at how much this little creature wanted to engage the world. Still, after two weeks I didn't think this merited actually taming the bird so I approached my neighbor and told him that I had only gotten as far as having her sit on my shoulder.

"What!? You've got to be kidding me!" was the reply. He was astounded that I had made any progress at all. Nonetheless, I asked if he wanted her back and the reply was an emphatic no! If I was willing to put up with Crazy Bird, I was more than welcome to it. I wasn't surprised. Happily, Ukie was mine.

Days and weeks went by and since my only responsibilities in life were to serve coffee and tame a shrew, Ukie and I had plenty of time together. Slowly she started to relax even more. We would sit and talk and she would fly around the apartment or ride on my shoulder. Once in awhile, she would allow me to hold her on the top of my hand, but only with no fingers protruding. Even then, she would stay there just briefly in order to get to my shoulder or head. Since I never clipped her wings, her preferred perch was the top of my head where she would make clumsy crash landings in my hair.

Sometimes she would overshoot me completely and land or collide into whatever happened to be behind me, at which time she would deliver a long scolding to whatever had gotten in her way, mostly inanimate objects like doors and furniture. It was like living in a war zone with a bright yellow heat sensitive missile swooping down on me from all angles.

She loved to get kisses and snuggle up to my face but never could I reach out with my hand to touch her. I was frustrated at this block but at the same time I had learned much about Ukie and I knew that this bird was a sweet and wonderful soul. She couldn't wait for me to get home and loved to ride around on my shoulder or on top of my head, constantly curious. She always had an opinion about everything I was doing.

One time, I wasn't paying attention and had situated myself in front of her cage while I sorted through a box of stuff. I was at it for a while before I realized that she had been very quiet. When I looked up I found that she had worked her way to the front of the cage to get as close as she could to try to see what was in the box and figure out what I was doing. She was so absorbed that she didn't notice me watching and nearly jumped out of her skin when I started to laugh.

Ukie was a wonderful companion during a time when I felt very alone. I was proud of the progress we had made. She taught me that no matter how small or large the animal, there is no difference in the attention and love required nor any limits to the emotions they are capable of sending back. Ukie radiated pure love and affection for me.

I did try to teach her to whistle and say a few words but Ms. Ukie was not having any of that. All her life she would be a relatively quiet bird except for her fine displays of hissy fits and squawks when she was not pleased. That was her auditory vocabulary. The other "words" or expressions she used became precious to me. She could say so much with her big round eyes and the plume on the top of her head. She would often sit looking up at the sound of my voice and her eyes would slowly blink and close, almost as if she were being hypnotized. When she was especially content she would swell up into a big ball of soft orange and yellow fluff, including even the little feathers on each side of her beak so that it looked like she was smiling. And she smelled so good. Her warm feathers emanated this wonderful scent that used to just draw me in.

Since she wasn't afraid of my face, I would often turn my head when she was puffed up this way on my shoulder and bury my nose in her feathers. She was so cozy, warm and soft. When we lived in California Ukie also proved to be a great earthquake alarm. Her system was so much more sensitive than mine and she could sense things long before I could. She always knew an earthquake was coming and would flap wildly around her cage for 30 to 60 seconds, giving me advanced warning whenever one was on its way.

Not long after adopting Ukie, I met a man and got engaged. Having been on my own for a while and experiencing a very tumultuous adolescence without much family support, I married too young and to someone I knew at the time was not the right person for me. But my need to belong to whatever kind of family unit I could find was very strong and at barely twenty years of age I married a man nine years my senior who had a young daughter from a previous marriage. The next eleven years were some of the hardest of my life. I was seeking and yearning to belong somewhere only to find myself even more alone in my marriage. But one thing always stayed with me: my love for animals, especially Ukie.

I remember on the night before my wedding, I had to move out of my apartment early and was sleeping on a sofa bed at a friend's house. For some reason in the middle of the night Ukie decided to take a trip around the room in the dark. I used to leave the door to her cage open and she always stayed put once the lights were out, but not that night. Maybe she was upset at the change of environment. Maybe she was trying to warn me of the difficult times ahead. I don't know.

But by the time all the flapping and crashing around had stopped, she was clinging to the back of the couch where I slept letting out a tirade of hisses and curses that seemed to go on forever. Sleepy as I was and having my own wedding to attend in just a few hours, I tried to talk soothingly to her and reach behind the couch to get her back into her cage. Well, of course by reaching my hand around between the couch and the wall all she could see were fingers coming at her and I got the one and only bite from Ukie that I would ever receive, and a hardy one at that!

Disgusted and failing miserably at my rescue attempt, I decided to let her stay there and went back to sleep with a throbbing finger. In the morning I moved the couch away from the wall and there she was, sitting on the floor. Sheepishly (for a bird) she hopped up onto my open hand. After sizing each other up for a few minutes, both of us decided it was best never to discuss the matter.

Eventually we had a breakthrough. It was about a year after getting married and around two years since acquiring her that Ukie and I were hanging out on the couch together one day, she sitting near my shoulder on one foot with the other tucked under her puffy ball of yellow feathers and me talking sweet nothings and giving kisses, when I once again reached out to try to touch her. This time for some reason, Ukie let me in. Maybe enough time had gone by or maybe she wasn't paying attention or maybe she was tired of hissing for the moment. But to my amazement, I found myself scratching and rubbing up under the feathers on the back of her head!

There was this scrawny boney neck under there with hard feather cones sprouting out of it. It felt funny to me, but to Ukie a whole new world had opened up. She was in absolute heaven. Before I knew it, she was turning her head this way and that so I wouldn't miss any spots.

Of course, every once in a while she'd have to pull away to give me one of her sneezy squawks, either to keep me in line or because I had accidentally turned a feather the wrong way but nevertheless the "scratchies" as I called it became part of our routine from then on. It was a landmark accomplishment. We eventually got to the point where she even liked to have the area around her beak and over her eyes and ears rubbed. This bird was a regular massage-a-holic. It became her favorite thing.

Her second favorite thing I discovered accidentally one day while I was washing the dishes. She had followed me into the kitchen and perched herself on the curtain rod above the kitchen sink. I was busy washing away when I heard some funny squeaks coming from above. When I looked up, at first I couldn't make out which end of Ukie I was looking at. She was hanging upside down with all her feathers fluffed and rolling her head around under her wings which were fully

extended, flapping away. It took me a minute to realize that
the sound of the water had made her want to take a bath.
Comical doesn't begin to describe it; she looked absolutely
loony. So after finishing the dishes, I found a shallow bowl
and filled it with warm water. She was timid at first, sitting on
the edge of the bowl but then she slid right in and started the
whole comedy routine all over again, flapping, squawking
with joy and rolling her head around under her wings. I got
the impression that instinct was telling her to do these things
but she couldn't quite get the hang of it.

Since she was a tropical bird, I knew that I shouldn't leave
her sitting around wet, so afterwards I would carry her into
the bathroom and set her up on a towel rod, and then gently
blow her dry with the hairdryer. She would sit with her eyes
closed and hold her wings out.

There's nothing like the feeling of meeting a mistreated
animal who thinks the world is a place in which to be angry,
fearful and alone and then to be able to show this wonderful
soul that the world does indeed hold love. Nothing in my life
has given me more satisfaction than this kind of experience
with an animal—watching them discover joy and comfort for
the first time. Maybe because in seeing their plight I have
also seen my own and just like them, I longed to have a place
to belong and to know that love was there. Ukie opened up
and became this calm, adoring companion with a huge
personality that I hardly suspected could be contained in such
a tiny body.

As the years passed more animals came into my life.
There are many feral cats wandering the streets of San Diego
and we had our share. A mother cat with her babies lived
under the house next to my apartment building along with
the neighborhood skunk! I started to feed these little ones
(the cats that is) and eventually adopted two of them.

Because of the new situation, Ukie had to be kept safely
in the bedroom and her life changed because of it. She did
not have the run of the house anymore or my undivided
attention. I felt torn. I could not resent my new feline

companions who had also struggled so much and whom I loved as I did Ukie. But it also wasn't fair to my dear friend who had come so far. I wished so much that they could all get along but it was impossible. I was in constant fear that the cats, who couldn't figure out why on earth I'd keep a bird and not eat it, would get to Ukie which they constantly tried to do. I did my best to give everyone enough attention but Ukie got the short end of the stick.

Unfortunately, the cats had both already contracted feline leukemia before I could rescue them off the street and one of them died shortly after I took them in. But the other cat, even though diagnosed with leukemia, continued to thrive.

Also around this time I realized that my marriage which had lasted a little over a decade, was ending. I found myself on a red-eye flight in May of 1994 from San Diego back to Rochester, New York where I had originated, with a cat in cargo and Ukie under my seat in a small cage. When the vet came to examine both cat and bird in order to issue health certificates for the flight, he reached in to take Ukie out of her cage and she latched onto the skin between his thumb and index finger. Thinking of the one time she had bitten me many years ago, I was a little alarmed.

But the vet, as if reading my mind said, "See how she's got me there? She could really do some damage right now but she's not, she's letting me know she doesn't like this but she doesn't want to hurt me." My little Ukie had truly come a long way. I felt so proud of her. She was an angel on the flight, completely calm and quiet except for take off and landing when she would squawk once. It was funny to watch people turn around looking for the source of the sound.

When we landed in Chicago around 3 a.m. I had a few hours to wait until my connection so I found an empty row of chairs, rolled my jacket up and used Ukie's little cage as a pillow. We took a long nap together.

Arriving in Rochester was like a homecoming for me. It had been almost seventeen years but I still recognized much of the city. Shortly after moving to New York, I met Brian who worked at the same university where I was employed as an interpreter. Brian was everything my ex-husband had not been: attentive, passionate, fun and adoring. I found the whole combination irresistible after so many years in an unhappy marriage and enjoyed for the first time in a long time or maybe ever, a relationship where I actually laughed and had fun.

To top the cake, Brian became fascinated with Ukie. He would go out and buy toys for her, even a whole play set that he put on top of her cage. He loved to take her out and watch her fly around or take a bath. I eventually brought Ukie over to his place since there she could be free and have the run of the house like she used to. He would always have her riding on his shoulder, always delighting in her company.

Ukie too was happy and didn't seem to have any problems with this new person in her life. Brian learned how to pick her up and how to respect her fear of fingers. He genuinely seemed to love her as I did. Unfortunately, after being together for a few years, Brian and I didn't get along quite as well as he and Ukie did, so after an especially bumpy time, we broke off the relationship. We were still on speaking terms, though, and it was then that I knew I had to make a very hard decision.

Do I take Ukie back, knowing that she'd once again have to be relegated to the spare room where I could only be with her minimally? Or do I give her the kind of life where she would be free to fly and have the companionship she deserves? By this time Ukie had been with me for fifteen years, I didn't know how much longer she might live and I wanted her to have the best life possible.

On the other hand, I felt so fortunate to have found someone who really loved her and had become so attached to her. What were the chances of finding Ukie such a good home? So, after many promises and reassurances from Brian, I decided to let her go.

A few years went by but I never forgot about my Ukie and always wondered how she was. Even though Brian and I had been on speaking terms at first, that was realistically hard to maintain after both of us started to see other people and eventually we lost contact. Then suddenly the cat I had brought with me from California succumbed to the leukemia she had been carrying around in her body all those years and died very quickly. I was devastated and it took a long time to heal from the pain and shock. But as I did, I started to wonder about Ukie, knowing that I was in a position now to give her my full attention once more. I thought about how exciting it would be to have her back, I wondered if she was even still alive. So I wrote a letter to Brain.

The response I received back was disappointing but heartening at the same time. He said that Ukie was indeed still around and she and Brian were still best buddies. He even stated that he wouldn't know what he'd do without her. Well, how could I refute that? Apparently I had made the right decision when I gave her up. I had to realize and accept that she truly belonged to someone else now and that she was happier as a result, but I still missed her and thought of her often.

Again, more time passed. I had also begun volunteering at a small and understaffed animal shelter in a rural town nearby. It was a joy to see things improving for these animals and as you can imagine, one side effect from regular shelter exposure was that I brought home a few new companions and found myself once again with two wonderful cats.

It was around this time that I had a dream about Ukie. I just remember that for some reason she was colored bright pink and flying towards me. She landed next to me, looked me straight in the eye and said, "Hi Mommy!"

This was interesting because even though I do think of my animal companions as my children I never referred to myself as Ukie's "mommy" specifically. And when she said these words, she emanated such a warm, loving and joyful energy towards me that when I woke up I was elated, knowing that this dream had to be from Ukie and that my girl held no grudges about my having given her up, that she loved me with all her heart.

But while I was very touched, I was also concerned. I dream often and my dreams tend to be very vivid and somewhat unusual. When I dream of getting a message such as the one I received from Ukie, it's usually after the soul has moved on from this life. Naturally I wondered if maybe this was such a farewell message. It had been a little over a year since I had contacted Brian and felt a little awkward contacting him again, but I had to know.

To my surprise the answer was that Ukie was alive and well, and would I like to have her back? I was astounded. Why now? What would I do with her and two cats? But I couldn't say no, this was my chance. Altogether it had now been 23 years and I was 41 years old. So much had happened and here was this small and wonderful bird who had been there through so much of it all and now I could have her back in my life! I jumped at the opportunity.

In the transaction of getting Ukie back to me, Brian had decided that he would send her via a friend instead of bringing her himself which I thought was a little strange. But when the car pulled into the driveway and I got my first look at Ukie in almost ten years I understood why. I was appalled at what I saw. There she was in the same cage with the same food dishes which were filthy and exactly the same toys as she had so long ago when I first gave her away.

The cage was rusty and unkempt. I hardly recognized her. Her feathers, which had always remained beautiful and full were soiled and she was hunched over. Her claws were so long she could barely hang on to the perch. She didn't recognize me but instead hissed and squawked as only Ukie could. Well, at least it was good to know some things never change. But you can imagine how I felt.

I was outraged, but Brian would have nothing to do with me. It was then that I realized the dream I had had of Ukie was no coincidence. At just the right time, Ukie had known that she needed to give me a tap on the shoulder. If it hadn't been for the dream I never would have checked again and I would not have gotten her back and saved her from the misery and loneliness she must have felt.

Over the next few weeks Ukie was given a new larger cage with larger perches wrapped in rubber gauze that she could hang onto without having to grip too hard. I also found small wire platforms where she could stand flat and not have to use her claws at all. She had new toys and mirrors to play with. I even devised a heating unit made from a reptile cage warming device attached to a glass oven plate that I tied onto the lower part of her cage so she would always be warm.

She could barely walk or hop anymore so everything in her cage had to be within reach. I did everything I could to make her comfortable. The vet had given her a shot of cortisone which would eventually wear off but it had provided some relief from the pain for a short time.

I tried to see if she wanted a bath but it was too difficult and such things really didn't hold much interest for her anymore. One activity though that we did reinstate as soon as she became used to my presence again was the "scratchies." She still loved to be rubbed all over her head. And thanks to some friends I knew who also owned birds and had much more experience than I did, we figured out that we could do the pruning that Ukie couldn't do for herself.

So slowly we would work our way through her feathers, peeling off the wax coating on each feather shaft with our fingernails letting the bright yellow plumage unfold until she somewhat resembled the beauty she once was, even though she could never really hold herself upright again.

I was working full time, had the two cats as well as many other responsibilities, but I tried to sit and visit with Ukie as much as I could. I set up a trickling water fountain in her room and had classical music CD's playing when I wasn't there to make sure she never felt alone again. When I was home she still loved to come out and be in the center of things as she used to.

But because she could no longer fly, I carried her around cradled in a blanket most of the time. She dealt with the inconvenience of her physical condition as gracefully as any elderly lady would. I observed in Ukie a wisdom that I realized she had always had--the ability to stay strong and accept situations even though they weren't the most comfortable or convenient. She must have been in a lot of pain but she still had that sweet spirit and that huge personality. She truly still was the same bird I had found so long ago on that rainy day. And even though many years had passed, here we were still relatively alone in the world except for each other. Things really hadn't changed that much.

About a year went by. Every morning when I would uncover Ukie's cage, part of me wondered if she would still be alive. I knew her time was short. We had now been together 24 years. Then one day I saw signs that she might be approaching the end. I called my other bird friends over and we gathered around her that evening. We talked about Ukie and all the great things she had done and all that she had lived through. She sat there in front of us on my coffee table wrapped in a blanket, her eyes closed, looking tired and faded. We thought she would go at any moment.

Then at one point I thought to give her some millet and to our surprise she rallied and started to munch away with renewed energy to which we were all amazed. I didn't know what that meant. Maybe she could go for another few days or weeks? I just didn't know. Ukie had staying power--there was no doubt about that.

The next morning, I uncovered her cage and there she was, looking back at me. What a relief. I took her out and held her for a while. She mostly slept. Then, after a few hours I knew I had to run some errands and I thought that maybe I should do that sooner than later, anticipating that it would be harder to leave as she deteriorated. It was a Saturday and I wanted to be around for the rest of the night and Sunday in case she needed me.

So I started to put her back in her cage. Right then Ukie opened her eyes wide and struggled to stay in my hand. She was using what little strength she had to let me know she didn't want me to go. I told her, "It's okay, baby. I'll be right back, I promise."

I put her down on the blanket above the heating unit in her cage with a little food and water within reach. As I left the room I had the thought that if she passed while I was gone on some silly errands which could have waited, I would never forgive myself.

About two hours later, I had finished up and was starting back when suddenly I felt a sense of urgency and I knew I had to get home. I tried to hurry, but it was too late. I ran into the house and found her up against the side of the cage where she had apparently wandered off of the blanket. She had gotten the side of her tiny body caught in the bars and couldn't get herself out.

Ukie was gone. She had needed me and I had not been there. My girl had died alone. After all those years and all that time apart, after Ukie reached out to me and I had gotten her back, after all of that, I left when she needed me the most. All I could think about was how special and precious it would have been to be right there with her when she passed--how much that would have meant for both of us. She knew, and she tried to tell me but I didn't listen and left anyway. I cried but inside my heart was numb. I couldn't bear to think about what had happened and how once again I had failed such a faithful friend.

I wanted so badly to go back and make a different choice, to give her that extra time that she deserved but didn't get. Of course we always tell ourselves that we can't know for sure, that we do the best we can about these things. But that just wasn't enough in this case. I should have been there. I wanted Ukie's story to have a different ending and I would have given anything to make that happen.

The guilt was overwhelming. I removed her from the cage. She hardly weighed a thing. I cradled her in my arms for a long time. I told her how sorry I was, how very sorry. But it was just too little too late. I thought about how these things are supposed to be. I wondered why life doesn't warn you when you're about to make a big mistake, and then I realized that it had. If I had listened to Ukie and to my instinct, my heart, I would have stayed no matter how long it took.

I removed the little silver ID band that she had had around her ankle all her life and remembered how she used to pull at it and how much it always annoyed her. I wondered why I hadn't removed it long before. I gathered as many feathers from the cage as I could. I had her cremated the next day.

I still have Ukie here with me, but now in a little tin container. And even though as I write this it's been almost three years, I still can't look at it without feeling regret and sorrow.

But her death was not the end. Ukie once more, as she had done in the past, reached out and sent a message. A few weeks after she died I had another dream.

I was standing on a street in front of a large brick building. I wasn't sure what I was doing there until someone that I couldn't see told me that in that building was Ukie with her new owner. Immediately I was concerned. What new owner? Who had her now?

Whoever it was, I was not about to trust anyone with my sweet little bird again. I went in and climbed a few flights of stairs before I came to an open door. I went inside and there in a small room was an old wooden desk with a radio on top of it and an empty chair. Behind the desk was a bird cage sitting on a stand, but it too was empty. I stood there for a moment looking around when someone walked in behind me. I turned to find a man standing there. Feeling upset and confused, I asked him where Ukie was and what was is this place? He told me not to worry.

He said, "This is my radio station and I'm the DJ here. Ukie sits in her cage behind me all day while I play classical music. She loves it and she's very happy. And if you tune into my station and listen very closely, you can even hear her singing along."

I woke up with tears streaming down my face. What a message, what a comfort! Here she was again, this time letting me know that she was doing just fine and would never be very far away. As usual, Ukie held no grudge and she cared enough to make sure that I knew it. She still loved me and wanted to help ease my guilt and grief.

I felt honored and grateful. I only hope in turn that she knows my life would never have been the same without her and I was never worthy of such an amazing and wonderful friend. I will never forget the lessons she taught me about friendship, love, loyalty and how to flow with life.

12 SHANTI: ANGEL IN TRAINING
By Sharon Jogerst

*"As winter stormed on, there were signs from the heavens that Shanti
would be going soon. One morning I awoke to a magnificent angel's
wing that appeared in frost overnight on the window right above the bed
where Shanti was sleeping. As the sun rose, it lit up the wing in a
brilliant gold and then to my amazement a rainbow appeared in the sky.
This was really strange because the temperatures were below zero and
there didn't seem to be anything that would cause a rainbow to appear
like that in the cold, winter sky."*

I believe that animals come to us as guides, as healers, as
teachers and as angels to protect us. They come disguised as
fur and flesh offering pure, unconditional love. I met Shanti
in the summer of 1992 and my world changed forever. She
came in the form of an innocent and helpless puppy who
reached out to me with soft, sensitive brown eyes and
wrapped herself around my heart. Little did I know then that
this small, red, fluffy puppy who looked like a baby fox would
become one of my greatest teachers. She would challenge me
to reach deep into my soul. She would teach me forgiveness
and propel me forward in my work as a healer.

On the day that I found Shanti, I was walking outdoors
on the Pearl Street Mall in Boulder, Colorado. It was a
sweltering day in July and I was on a lunch break from work.
All at once, I came upon two tiny, tar-covered, thin and

bedraggled puppies tied up to a post and left in the hot sun. I only noticed them because as I walked past, the little red foxy one cried out to me with pleading eyes and a small desperate bark. She was obviously a little Chow mix, but with very fine features. Tied next to her was a sweet Australian Shepherd puppy with a blue eye and a brown eye who was also looking desperate, but hopeful. I walked over to them and instantly realized how hungry and thirsty they both were. I had a sandwich in my hand that I had planned to eat for lunch, so I gave each puppy a half of my sandwich. They ate ravenously and I gave them water as well. I asked the people at the nearby kiosk if they knew anything about the puppies. They told me someone had tied them up early in the morning and never came back for them. I asked them if they would mind bringing water to the puppies throughout the day as I was going to have to return to work. They said that they would. I returned to work and for the rest of the day, I couldn't stop thinking about the two puppies.

Later that evening I returned to the mall after work, with my husband, Joe. I couldn't believe my eyes. The puppies were still there, seven hours later. By this time they were just lying still, lethargic and dehydrated from the heat. A crowd of concerned people had gathered and a police officer was also there. He said that he couldn't do anything about the puppies because they were tied up legally. Soon a woman from the Humane Society showed up. After assessing the situation, she determined that if there was somebody in the crowd who wanted to take the puppies, then they should take them. I spoke up immediately and Joe went to get the van. We loaded up the two very tired precious puppies and drove them to our little house in the mountains.

My mind was racing on the way home. First of all, "What was I doing rescuing a Chow mix puppy? Only a year before this, four red Chows had killed two of my goats and seriously injured a third one. I had a thing against Chows, especially red Chows. I realized that this innocent puppy was offering me a lesson in forgiveness. I could continue to hold a grudge against all Chows or I could go into my heart and realize that this little puppy had nothing to do with any of my past grievances. She needed me so badly. I was her lifeline. She softened my heart and I became eternally devoted to her.

I was planning to find homes for both of the puppies because we were renting a very small house in Gold Hill, Colorado and already had two large golden retrievers, Tuza and Girlie, as well as a grey Russian Blue kitty, Zachariah. When we arrived home, Tuza and Girlie were waiting for us and were very excited to have the puppies there. Tuza and Girlie had been parents before, having had two litters of puppies together. Zachariah accepted the pups as well, as long as they left his food bowl alone. We gave the puppies food and water and they ate and drank eagerly. Then they fell fast asleep with full bellies.

The following day, we asked around the neighborhood to see if anybody wanted a puppy. We found a home for the Australian Shepherd pup and then a friend of mine from work asked to take the little red Chow mix. Everything was set except for the fact that by this time I had fallen so deeply in love with this puppy that I realized I just couldn't let her go. I went to talk to my landlord to see what he would say about my keeping a third dog in that tiny house. He said to my utter delight, "Of course the baby can stay." I was elated. I decided to call her Shanti which means "peace." This began our life together.

When I took Shanti to the vet the following day, he determined that she was not more than five weeks old, too young to be weaned. She was malnourished and full of worms. With loving care we nursed her back to health. She grew quickly and Tuza and Girlie were wonderful parents to her. They were both ten years old by this time and no longer very agile. Because of this, Shanti assumed that she must be the fastest dog in the whole world. She would run like the wind and was so proud that nobody could catch up to her. Girlie taught her to swim which wasn't really her nature, but she wanted to do everything that Girlie did. Shanti quickly became a great swimmer. She was a little red Chow mix being raised as a Golden Retriever.

I soon realized that there was something different about Shanti's nature that I had never encountered in a dog before. I had always had Golden Retrievers and had trained and showed dogs in obedience from the time I was seven years old. I was used to the Golden Retriever nature, so eager to please, easy to train because they love and trust most everybody. Shanti was different. Shanti had a mind of her own and I would need to learn to work with her using gentleness, love and respect. She was not the kind of dog I could just tell to do my bidding and expect her to obey me. She would only do things on her terms. She reminded me of the fox in the book, *The Little Prince* by Antoine de Saint Exupery. I was going to have to "tame" her first and win her heart with trust and love.

Shanti was extremely sensitive. This was something I learned to be aware of at all times. The more time I spent with her, the more sensitive I became. She was very shy and didn't trust people in general, especially men. She didn't like loud noises and she was afraid of many things. She would especially cower when she saw a man in a baseball cap carrying a guitar. I figured this had something to do with her experience as a very young, desperate puppy.

I soon learned also that Shanti had strong separation anxiety. She needed to have me constantly in her sight. Although she was always accompanied by Tuza and Girlie, if I left her in the car while doing an errand, she would squeeze herself through the tiniest opening in the window and come in search of me. I couldn't imagine how she managed to get through some of the spaces she got through without injuring herself. This made it very difficult to take her with me, especially when it was hot outside. When I would leave her at home, even with Joe there, Shanti would go into utter depression and exile herself until my return. Joe would be unable to find her or coax her out. Only the other dogs would know where she was and would run to get her to let her know when I came home.

Although Shanti demanded a great deal of attention and I needed to be constantly attuned to her emotional well-being, Shanti gave me a kind of love in return that I have never experienced before. She was concerned about my every move. She watched me like a hawk and worried about me any time I was out of her sight. She was my protector. I've never felt such devotion and unconditional love pouring out to me in a steady stream. We became telepathically connected. I knew her thoughts and she knew mine. We were absolutely crazy about each other.

Shanti had some wonderful years with Tuza and Girlie. They were a family and Shanti was their baby. We often went out to Lake Powell in Utah together, swimming in the incredible azure water and hiking the mystical canyons.

After a few years, Joe and I bought a little A-frame cabin near Estes Park, Colorado. It was on three acres surrounded by National Forest, teeming with wildlife. We had bears visiting us daily as well as foxes, coyotes and an occasional mountain lion. Although we had a fence around our property, the dogs and our kitty had to be much more careful and aware of their surroundings in these woods and they depended on each other to be on the lookout and keep each other safe.

Tuza and Girlie were getting on in years. Our dear, sweet Girlie passed away at age fifteen. Beloved Tuza passed away a year later at the ripe old age of sixteen. Shanti grieved their passing deeply. It was especially hard after Tuza was gone. For the first time, Shanti didn't have another dog around. This threw her into a kind of confusion and insecurity, along with her apparent grief.

I knew that Shanti needed another dog companion. I could tell that she felt very vulnerable and there was an immense sadness in her eyes. She was so sad, she could barely swallow. Shanti and I set out together to find a new friend for her. We went to The Humane Society in Boulder first, and with every dog that I brought out to meet her, she would just hide her head in my lap and ignore it. The next place I took her, "Every Creature Counts," she did the same thing. She refused to even acknowledge the other dogs. So we went back home without a new friend and Shanti's grief continued.

About a week later, I was in Denver, visiting my father. I saw his newspaper lying on the table and picked up the ad section and looked under "Pets." There was an ad that caught my eye. It read, "Sundance, the most loving dog in the world needs a home...one and a half year old, male golden retriever." I called the number and a woman named Cheryl answered. She said I was at least the 100th caller and she had told everyone before me that the dog had been taken. She liked my voice and the fact that I lived in the mountains and had another dog, so she invited me to come and meet Sundance.

When I came up to the porch at the house, Sundance met me at the door and from that point forward, stuck to me like glue. He was a big, powerful golden retriever, weighing in at 85 pounds. My first thought was that he was bigger than I was looking for as far as fitting into the car easily, plus our house was so tiny. It was obvious, however, that Sundance had every intention of coming home with me, and Cheryl had already decided that I was the one she chose to take Sundance. She was having a really hard time giving him up. She loved him dearly. However, she had recently moved in with her boyfriend who had two male Rottweilers. They were bullying Sundance mercilessly and he had a serious injury from being bitten on the head. So, I decided to take Sundance home with me to meet Shanti.

The moment I drove up with Sundance in the car, Shanti was ecstatic. She let out a yelp of delight. Sundance was also very excited. They couldn't wait to be together. I let him into the backyard and instantly they were playing together. Shanti suddenly realized how big he was and let out a fearful cry. Sundance understood and immediately got down on his belly so he could play with her at her own level. From that moment forward, they were inseparable, the very best of friends. Sundance was strong and athletic. He gave Shanti a feeling of security. They did everything together: hiking, swimming, traveling in the car, and the happiest times were the ones spent at Lake Powell out on our boat.

Shanti needed a dog like Sundance because her highly sensitive nature made her fearful. Her greatest fear was what came to be known as "The Snow Monster." In the winter when we would get a lot of snow, after a snowstorm, the sun would come out and begin to melt the snow. The snow on the steep A-frame roof would shift and slide off in sheets, making a kind of deep, groaning sound as it moved. Shanti was absolutely terrified by this sound. She would tremble all over and hide all day from the Snow Monster. This made winters tough on her, poor girl. Eventually we moved from that house and the Snow Monster was never heard from again.

We moved to our dream house with lots of room on several acres at the edge of the National Forest. The first winter after we moved there, we made friends with a very special little red fox. He was very friendly and tame and often came to the window to look in at us. We decided to call him Foxy. The interesting thing about Foxy was that he looked very much like Shanti, an alter ego perhaps. Shanti and Sundance accepted Foxy's presence completely. They would often lie on either side of the sliding glass door with Foxy on the outside and Shanti and Sundance on the inside. We soon learned that Foxy had a mate, a beautiful red fox with a very positive attitude who skipped wherever she went. She was a little shier, but very sweet. We call her Roxy. I was always puzzled how Shanti accepted the foxes so readily, when normally she wouldn't even accept other dogs being around. There was something mystical about their presence. They seemed like protectors. Could this be the reincarnation of Tuza and Girlie coming back to look in on the little puppy they had raised? I wondered.

As time went on, Shanti and Sundance enjoyed lots of

great hikes in the mountains and beautiful days swimming at Lake Powell. When Shanti was about twelve years of age, however, I noticed that she was starting to limp on her front right leg. At first it seemed to be related to exercise so I would try to make sure she didn't overwork herself and got plenty of rest. Unfortunately, the limping continued to get worse and out of necessity the hikes got shorter and shorter.

I was really bothered by Shanti's deteriorating condition and I started to do whatever I could to help relieve her pain. I took her to the vet and he diagnosed that Shanti had an arthritic elbow. He prescribed some anti-inflammatory medication which helped only a little bit. I am a Massage Therapist by trade so I naturally started to work on Shanti.

I started to massage her daily and also began to give her glucosamine for her joints. She was still not doing well with her right front leg and by this time was holding it out in front of her when she walked, using only three legs. I decided to try using hot stone massage on her as I had achieved great results when using hot stones on my human clients. To my utter amazement, after the first treatment Shanti started walking on all four legs again. I continued with the treatments and also began using an infrared healing lamp on her. This also seemed to help a lot in making her more comfortable.

For the next couple of years, Shanti held her own, but sadly was unable to go for hikes like she used to. Her arthritis got gradually worse and started to affect all of her joints. Her back legs were not holding her up very well. When we took her to Lake Powell, she would still enjoy swimming, but would spend the rest of her time sleeping in her bed on the boat.

Swimming was very therapeutic for her as she was able to move and exercise all of her muscles without putting any weight or stress on her joints. It was like flying for her. I would always notice after coming home from Lake Powell, she would be moving so much better after swimming every day for a week.

When Shanti was fourteen years old, we came back from a trip to Lake Powell and Shanti seemed to be doing very well. She was happy and eating well and had just gone to lie down outside after dinner. Because it was dusk and I always like to have the dogs in at this time because this is when the mountain lions are most active, I asked Joe if he could call Shanti in. When he went outside to call her in, in one instant she went from being fine, to being very ill. Just as she lay down, her stomach had twisted inside of her and she began to bloat. Joe called me and I recognized instantly that Shanti was in serious condition. There was a horrible gurgling sound coming from her stomach which was expanding at an alarming rate. I called the emergency veterinarian clinic in Boulder and informed them we were coming immediately. It was a half hour drive to Boulder. We loaded Shanti in the car and drove there as quickly as possible. I sat in the back with Shanti, encouraging her and reassuring her, but my heart was sinking. Was I going to lose my little girl in this way?

When we got to the vet they explained that Shanti would need immediate surgery. If it wasn't too late, there was a chance for her to recover. If too much time had passed, however, the stomach tissue would begin to die and Shanti would be unable to survive. I was distraught. I didn't want to put a fourteen year old dog through surgery and I was also very aware of Shanti's arthritis and limitations. Perhaps it was time to let her go. The vet told me that I had only four minutes to make a decision. I told Joe about my concerns but he felt really strongly that we should at least give her a chance. I felt in my heart that Shanti wanted to survive and continue her life with us. We told the vet to go ahead and do the surgery. The vet said that she would be able to tell more once she opened Shanti up and if things weren't looking good, she would put Shanti down and Shanti just wouldn't wake up.

Joe and I left the vet's office with very heavy hearts. We went home not knowing what the outcome would be. The vet said she would call us as soon as she was done with the surgery. At about two o'clock in the morning, the vet called with good news. Everything went very well with the surgery and Shanti was going to pull through. I was so relieved.

Shanti had a couple of rough days after she came home, but she recovered very quickly. Foxy and Roxy seemed to know that something was wrong. They were there to greet Shanti when she came home and were very concerned about her, keeping a steady watch on her from a distance. Before long, Shanti was back to her old self and the vet said it would be okay for her to swim again.

We took one last trip to Lake Powell that year and Shanti did wonderfully. She swam a lot and slept on the boat when she was tired. That was to be her last trip to Lake Powell with us.

When we got home from Lake Powell, I noticed once again that Shanti was moving so much better after having had the chance to swim for a week. I realized then that in order to keep Shanti comfortable, I needed to find a place for her to swim regularly. Winter was setting in and I knew Shanti wouldn't do well unless she could somehow swim. I looked in the phone book and found a facility called "Back on Track." I called the number and a very friendly voice answered. Her name was Susie and she ran a rehabilitation center for dogs who were recovering from surgery, dogs who had suffered a stroke or dogs with arthritis. She told me she had a dog pool where Shanti could swim. I scheduled an appointment for the very next day.

The swimming experience at "Back On Track" was somewhat different than Shanti was used to. Upon arrival, she was suited up with a life vest and then lifted into a pool of warm water. The pool was actually a tank that was only about four feet deep. A leash was attached to the life vest and held while Shanti swam in place. Susie wanted to break Shanti in slowly and the first day she only swam four minutes. I was a little bit bothered by this because I knew that Shanti could swim so much longer. Every time we went though, the time was increased by a few minutes. The goal was for Shanti to become a member of "The 30 Minute Club." There was a bulletin board on the wall with pictures of all the dogs who were members of the "30 Minute Club." Shanti swam twice a week and within a couple of months she too became an honorary member of the club. She holds the record to this day of being the oldest dog ever to become a member of "The 30 Minute Club."

As winter progressed, Shanti suffered some setbacks. She was losing strength in her hind legs and took a couple of bad falls. After that, she was no longer able to climb or go down the stairs by herself. Shanti decided in her own mind that if she could no longer walk, then she might as well fly. She began to literally throw herself off the stairs or out of the car door. Wherever she wanted to go, she would try to fly there. This is when I realized that my dear, precious, beloved Shanti was now an "angel in training" and our time together on earth was drawing to a close.

In the last months of her life, I spent all of my time with Shanti. I carried her up and down the stairs and continued to give her massage treatments on a daily basis. By this time she was swimming three times a week for it was only in the water that she was truly free from pain and limitations. I increased her pain medication as well to try to keep her more comfortable. I knew that somehow I was going to have to prepare myself to say good-bye and I just couldn't imagine my life without her. She was so much a part of me.

As winter stormed on, there were signs from the heavens that Shanti would be going soon. One morning I awoke to a magnificent angel's wing that appeared in frost overnight on the window right above the bed where Shanti was sleeping. As the sun rose, it lit up the wing in a brilliant gold and then to my amazement a rainbow appeared in the sky. This was really strange because the temperatures were below zero and there didn't seem to be anything that would cause a rainbow to appear like that in the cold, winter sky.

A few days after the angel's wing appeared on the window, I received in the mail, out of the blue, a little, white stuffed dog with angel's wings. It was a random gift of appreciation from an animal welfare group that I make donations to. I knew this was another sign that my angel dog, Shanti, would be leaving soon.

As weeks passed by, Shanti was having more and more difficulty getting around. I was still taking her swimming three times a week and she could still swim thirty minutes, but at home she lay on her bed most of the time.

I was starting to really struggle with the question of whether or not Shanti still had a good quality of life and if I should assist her in passing on. Joe and I discussed it a lot and we went back and forth. Some days she had good days, other days were not good at all.

Finally Shanti began to show signs of being seriously ill so Joe and I made the decision that it would be best to call the vet and make an appointment to help her pass on. But on the day that we decided to make the call, I just couldn't bring myself to do it. I was trying to convince myself that maybe she would get better. I just wanted one more day.

The following morning, I opened my eyes and sat up to look at Shanti. As I gazed at her, she woke up and looked back at me. What passed between us in that moment was almost indescribable. The love was so profound, so intense and reached far beyond the physical here and now. She looked like she had resolved herself to the inevitable. I picked her up gently and carried her into the yard to do her morning business.

At this point, Shanti began to cry out in pain. She was bleeding internally as a result of the pain medication. Sundance came to her and licked and licked her face. He knew she was very ill and he was saying good-bye. Joe and I picked her up and put her on her bed and then carried her to the car. Foxy and Roxy were there also, looking very concerned and they both lay down next to the car. We had to get them out of the way before we could leave.

It was a short ten minute ride to the vet. Everything seemed very surreal. When we got there, the vet came out to the car and determined that Shanti was bleeding internally. There was really nothing to be done except to assist her in passing on to the next realm. Joe and I said our good-byes and then the vet put her to sleep there in the car in her little bed. Her passing was very loving and peaceful.

When the vet picked up her limp, little body to carry her away, there was a tear in his eye. He had taken care of Shanti when she was only five weeks old and now at fifteen she had reached the end of her life. As he carried her away, she looked so relaxed and it was good to know that she was no longer in pain.

Driving home from the vet, I had the feeling one has when driving home from the airport after dropping off a loved one. Shanti was on her way. She was now truly an angel.

That night I had a profound dream. Shanti was there with me—one hundred percent in flesh, bone and fur. I spent the whole night in my dream with her, petting her and holding her, marveling at how she was still there with me, so complete and whole.

Two days later, I decided to take Sundance to the dog park. We were both grieving together and I felt that he needed to see some other dogs. When we got to the dog park, there were a lot of dogs there and Sundance was playing with them. Soon, however, all the dogs left and suddenly it was like I was standing in a dream. I turned around and right at my feet was a little Chow mix looking up at me. She was the spitting image of Shanti! Sundance began to play with her and I was transported into a timeless realm as I watched them play together. It was like watching Shanti and Sundance play together years ago when they first met. I still can't explain how this manifestation somehow happened before me. Perhaps for an instance, Shanti was able to borrow this body to help Sundance and me in our healing process. It seemed like a miracle.

The next night in my dream I found Shanti waiting for me, lying as close as she could to me at the door between our worlds. She was letting me know that she was still there. After weeks past, I was still grieving and missing Shanti so much that I had fallen into a kind of depression. I realized then that I still had pictures on my digital camera that I had taken but never seen. I decided to print the pictures that were there.

To my amazement there were pictures of the angel's wing with the rainbow that had appeared above Shanti's bed in the winter. There were also some pictures that Joe had taken of Shanti in the snow. When I looked at the pictures of Shanti in the snow, my heart skipped a beat.

There were several indistinguishable orbs surrounding Shanti. I have heard that angels sometimes travel in the shape of an orb that can sometimes be caught on film. My dear, little, Shanti had been surrounded by angels!

Finally I have peace in my heart. I feel the universe has spoken to me in so many ways to let me know that Shanti is okay. I know that our bond of love will go on into eternity, and in whatever way she can, Shanti my soul mate will always be with me.

13 BAT SHIT CRAZY
By Ingrid Collins

"Ella, my spirit medium client, was a fascinating woman who often gave me a running commentary about the glorious souls in Spirit who were working with me as healing messengers. Now, through my hot tears and grieving heart, and although I wanted desperately to turn back the clock, I knew that this was the time for Moonbeam's departing.

"Her companion is in place," Ella, said. "She is also a cat, the same type as her, but darker and with an unusual, unpronounceable name. She says she's one of yours."

I squealed with delight at her contact with Pyewacket, my boisterous, raucous, seal-point Siamese friend. Ella went on to say, "Usually, a companion waits about a metre above the head but, how odd, she is crouching only about six inches above her, focusing intently on her."

"That's definitely Pye. She was very near-sighted."

"It won't be long now, Ingrid," sighed Ella, standing at the door of my consulting room. We had finished our session and Ella was just leaving, her hand resting on the doorknob. She had said her gentle goodbyes minutes earlier to Moonbeam, our hauntingly beautiful old blue-point Siamese cat, as she lay sleeping by her side on her favourite cushion, the smoky grey blue of her almost foxlike face, alert ears, slim, elegant paws and long whip of a tail contrasting subtly with the cream of the rest of her fur.

In true feline tradition, as with all her ancestors and

inheritors, Moonbeam had the knack of seeking out the sunniest spaces in her territory. Our home, a large terrace house in a leafy suburb of North London, faces west. The sun in the morning rises to greet us for breakfast and warms the back of the house and garden until midday, when it travels, followed by its handmaidens the cats, to send its fire, light and warmth in through my consulting room windows at the front of the house in the afternoon. Afternoon is the cat's sleeping period. Better to express their devotion to the hedonistic comforts this life affords, our cats choose to bestow their companionship at this part of the day by joining in afternoon client sessions whilst snoozing, often emitting musically rhythmic snores.

As evening approaches and the square patterns of sunlight flow stealthily down from where they have been warming the cushions, travelling along the carpet until they touch the foot of my desk at the other end of the room, so the cats will also end up in a cosily satisfied, deep-breathing heap there too, having magically manifested themselves there, imperceptibly, without overtly waking up to move position.

Moonbeam had won our love in so many ways. People who live with Siamese cats know that they have the knack of meeting you in an enchanted space that is neither cat nor human but half way in between. Long before I met my dear friend Amelia, who has empowered me to speak out about these things, it was this powerfully psychic cat who had taught me the secret joys of receiving thoughts, images and words by telepathy. As spoken language is our way of manifesting and communicating our thoughts, telepathy with an individual from another species occurs at the pre-linguistic level in the pure energy form of thought. Our brains interpret and translate it into the language we ourselves speak.

Usually, Moonbeam's messages served to warn me of yet another mischief that her daughter Zizie was up to, with a gentle plea for my clemency: "She is scratching the furniture in the lounge. She can't help it. Be kind." or "My daughter ran into the basement when you went down there and you weren't looking. She knows she's not allowed in there, and you shut the door when you came out. Now she's locked in and says to tell you she wants to come out please." A bright accompanying picture would appear on all I can describe as like a cinema screen in my head, the little rascally rapscallion sitting intently close up to the inside of the basement door, her head up, blue eyes narrowed, and sweet lilac nose pointed purposefully at the door nob.

When Moonbeam had an important secret to tell me, she would sit and tap her paw on my knee to attract my attention and then, with her eyes shining like sunlight on water, she would search through the wavelengths until she hit on mine. We reveled in our secret communication, Moonbeam and I, because everyone knows for a fact that humans can't telepath with cats, Right? Right! Hush, but we know differently. Don't tell!

At times, wanting my attention when I was busily engaged in some boringly human activity that, to Moonbeam's mind, served no useful purpose, she would silently beam hot, loving rays of energy from her heart into my back until I became aware of her as a towering powerhouse of affection, and I would spin around! She would then shout in triumph at having achieved her goal and skip triumphantly into my arms. She was so right, of course. Stroking and tumbling with a passionate cat is a much more important activity than whatever I had been previously doing.

Some thoughts however she didn't need to telepath, because she was the greatest mime artist ever - I'm sure she taught Marcel Marceau, the famously original French mime artist all he knew. Lying on her back, a sexy wiggle, three paws curled and floppy but her right front paw held high in the air waving at me, this was always her blue-chip, top-of-the-range, super-duper, money-back-guaranteed ruse to bring me laughing to my knees. I'd join her on the carpet in a cuddle and squeaking match.

As with all Siamese, you gladly could lose yourself in the azure intensity of her iridescent blue eyes. She was a moon sprite, a mini goddess of the night, and she had taken my heart from the moment when, as a lively, curious and confident kitten, she had separated herself from her sisters and brothers, clambered nimbly up my shin and onto my lap to chew my necklace and claim me as her special friend. That distant spring evening all those long years ago she had slept contentedly on my lap, her tiny, furry head and delicate ears so weightless and warm in the palm of my left hand, my right hand caressing her creamy white, velvety fur for two bumpy hours as my husband Nick drove us so carefully back home to London from her mother's house by the sea.

Ella, my spirit medium client, was a fascinating woman who often gave me a running commentary about the glorious souls and celestials in Spirit who were working with me as healing guides and messengers. Sometimes she despaired of my irreverence in the presence of these helpers, but had to admit that they enjoyed a giggle, too.

Now, through my hot tears and grieving heart, and although I wanted desperately to turn back the clock, I knew that this was the time for Moonbeam's departing. She had become a serenely grand old lady with smiling memories of the coquettish kitten who had first appeared to me like a hazy wisp of light on a memorable, sea-breeze-anointed June day. This particular afternoon in the unforgiving present followed a week or so in which Moonbeam, old, tired and ill, had gradually refused food and drink - much longer than it was felinely possible for her to survive. Ella, from her vantage point at the door described the preparations for her departing. "Her companion is in place. She is also a cat, the same type as her, but darker and with an unusual, unpronounceable name. She says she's one of yours."

I squealed with delight at her contact with Pyewacket, my boisterous, raucous, seal-point Siamese friend (her mission: to chew as many pretty ribbons off my carelessly strewn nightgowns and negligées as possible before being apprehended and court marshaled) who had made the journey into Spirit through death about twenty years before.

With astonishingly cerulean sky eyes beaming laughingly out from her dark, mink-shiny face, Pye had taught me such games, which have been taken up by every subsequent one of our cats to the accompaniment of stereophonic purring - the favourite game is called Cuddle Me Up The Stairs, with variations.

Ella went on to say, "Usually, a companion waits about a metre above the head but, how odd, she is crouching only about six inches above her, focusing intently on her."

"That's definitely Pye. She was very near-sighted."

"Pyewacket is showing me that she has prepared a beautiful, sunny, grassy place for them both to live and play, surrounded by flowers. Moonbeam will be happy and will come over tomorrow."

Emma's words were true, and my beloved friend left me the next day to frolic in her special green place with my lovely old buddy Pyewacket, who all those years before had taken a part of my heart with her when she died. Knowing that she was going to live with Pye and have such eternal fun made it easier for me to say goodbye and allow her to go.

Moonbeam had given us a daughter, Zizie, and this little girl was the most magical of cats. A perfect little lilac-point, her pretty, permanently smiley face and pert ears, her busy paws and emotionally expressive tail were a pale, softly pinkish, mushroom brown. The cream of the rest of her beautiful little body shone, sparkled with light and, where her mother's eyes were that infinite azure, hers were the colour of Sri Lankan sapphires. One of my clients, the very talented young fashion designer Maria Grachvogel, called her "the Cindy Crawford of the cat world."

Zizie knew she was gorgeous and played on the fact—especially when she remembered that there was cold chicken or duck in the fridge just waiting to be donated into a worthy dish. In those instances, she would sit beside the fridge, one front paw held droopily up, head to one side, sighing audibly and looking utterly, glossily dejected. No way for one moment could she convince you that she was starving, but she looked so wonderfully sad that she invariably achieved her aim. Result! Back of the net! Her job in the home was that of court jester, always bringing smiles and laughter to us at times when we needed them most. She was a perennial, playful kitten right up to the end of her very long life. Her expertise lay in the fact that, should there have been a competition of the sort, she would have been able to purr for England as our national champion and Olympic gold medalist. She was a virtuoso and had many variations: purring while talking; purring while hiccoughing; purring while coughing; Tibetan over-purring, soprano purring, basso purring, sleeping whilst purring, and so on...

She also had an amazingly long memory: every spring, on the first day of the year warm enough for us to emerge and spend lazing in our garden, she would remind us of the Great Garden Grass Game. We had invented it one lazy, hot Sunday afternoon when she was a few months old. I had picked a long blade of couch grass and tickled her cute little nose with it, and the chase was on! How she skipped as she chased that long blade of grass, until eventually I grew tired of waving it around. Zizie yelled for more and that day we played until my arm was ready to fall off. After that, whenever we went out into the garden, which as you can imagine was very often, she would run up to the nearest blade of couch grass, bat it with her paw and cry piteously until I picked it and played the G.G.G.Game once more. Apart from the obvious pleasure of sharing her games, just to feel the urgent force of her vibrant forehead nuzzling in my hand was exquisite joy! To be her friend, to connect so directly heart to heart, soul to soul, was such a true privilege for me.

Every human companion of a cat will wax lyrical about how special their cat is - let's face it folks, the cat is a very unique creation who knows just the right buttons to press to ensure she has a meal ticket for life - but Zizie did me a service that I am sure was her mission on Earth for me. At one stage, when she was nine years and had never had a day's illness, she caught a kidney infection, developed kidney failure and was, the vet assured me, dying. I had just started my own private practice, having previously been a Consultant Educational Psychologist with the Inner London Education Authority until it was abolished in 1990 by Mrs. Thatcher's government. Although I had been offered a couple of tempting jobs in the devolved London boroughs - one in Camden and the other in Westminster—I had decided to go out on my own and at the beginning I was working solely from home. It was much later that I decided to take my practice into The London Medical Centre in Harley Street, this city's exclusive, famous medical neighbourhood.

A new client had been referred to me for therapy, a delightful young property developer called Fru, whom Zizie immediately claimed as a friend. She woke up from her fitful sleep when Fru arrived for her first session, shouted, "Weouuuuw!" and jumped on her knee. Apparently, Fru was used to being accosted by sick animals. She smilingly recalled a typical example when she was swimming in the sea and a dog had paddled out to her, swum around her, hitting her with his paws until she followed him back to the beach, where he had demanded healing. His human had been embarrassed and amazed. Yes, he had been in a road accident and was still not totally well. He was now, after Fru had treated him.

Fru stroked my insistent cat and, as her hands passed over Zizie's kidneys, she asked, "Do you know this cat is very ill? Have you taken her to the vet?"

"Yes," I replied, amazed at my first encounter with a spiritual healer. "The vet gave us antibiotics which cleared up the infection but left her with permanently damaged kidneys, so now she tells us it is a matter of a very short time before the end. When Zizie's quality of life becomes intolerably poor we will have to take her back to the surgery for her to be put down." I was near to tears and not at this stage feeling like a good therapist should feel in a client session.

"Please let me work on her whilst we talk?" asked Fru. My little cat was standing on her knee and bellowing up into

her face, obviously telling her just to get on with it; this is
what she had come for so, come on, show Ingrid what
spiritual healing is about. How much longer did she have to
suffer this pesky condition? Fru's hands started to move over
Zizie as we talked. As I later learned to do, here she was,
acting as a bridge for spiritual healing energy to flow from
Spirit through her own human energy field, or aura, to Zizie.
Every session after that, until she was cured about a couple of
months later, Zizie would wait at the storm doors three or
four minutes before Fru arrived for her appointment. She
would then lead the way into the consulting room, her
question mark tail in flag pole position, and take up her place,
luxuriating on her healer's lap and enjoying her energy
treatment, the clever little cat.

I had been such a rigorously trained scientist, graduating
from Manchester University with an Honours Degree as
Bachelor of Science. Yet here in my own home I was
witnessing the magic of fairy tales, but practical magic that
was slowly returning my beautiful cat to me in full health
before my astonished eyes. I realised that my client and my
cat were much wiser than I, and much more aware of the
dimension that my trembling soul now began to awake and
remember from childhood. My dear Fru took no prisoners.
She wanted to know why I was just "piddling around on the
surface using words?" She challenged me: why didn't I open
to Spirit and get on with the work I was destined to do?
"You have a great gift. I'm never wrong about these things.
Use it!"

A long story would follow here but that is for another
time when, relaxing with old friends late into the evening
after a very good meal and even better wine, we start retelling
to each other, a little tearfully, the story of our lives. Suffice it
to say, dear reader, I stopped piddling around on the surface
and I did open and get on with it. I established a thriving
practice and training clinic, The Soul Therapy Centre, that
thankfully both exist to the present day, and along the way I
have had some incredibly beautiful experiences of how our

animal friends make the journey from Spirit to communicate with us when we are at our most vulnerable, most in need of their warmth, their healing and their undying love.

With your permission, I would like to tell you the stories of some of these shining animal souls and their compassion.

Moonbeam returns

Whilst Zizie was still physically with us and her mother Moonbeam had died, we became aware that Zizie had taken to running around the house and garden, meowing soulfully. That was doubly heart-rending. We grieved for our beautiful and loving blue beauty, and felt helpless to comfort her daughter in her equally immense loss. Shortly afterwards, I had organized a workshop one evening at The Soul Therapy Centre on spirit mediumship. The presenter was the fabulously gifted medium, Marie Taylor. At the end of the evening with the group of participants, she had built up such a powerhouse of energy that we caused a table to move by transforming its physical matter into pure energy which we experienced as liquid energy beneath our fingers.

This is a riveting phenomenon to take part in. A small three-legged table is used a little like a ouija board, being placed in the centre of the group. A few of the more powerful psychics are chosen to come into the centre and put their fingertips lightly on the rim, transferring energy from their aura to the solid wood of the table top.

We are taught in school that all physical matter is made up of atoms, which in turn are made of sub-atomic particles. We now understand, with the aid of our advanced instrumentation, that these particles are infinitesimally small packets of energy in constant motion. By connecting ourselves in energetic state to the seemingly solid table, also in its energetic state, the table can be caused to move and it becomes a vehicle for Spirit. Three legs makes it more able to destabilize and travel, spinning around to the group members sitting in the circle.

This particular evening, establishing a simple alphabetic

code, the table spelt out messages for various p
Then the table practically flew off the ground a
centre of the circle. Those who were there tha
remember realising that Zizie had entered the 1
walked in to the centre of the circle. The table swayed gently
over her. It spelled out the letters M, O, O, N, B.... whilst
Zizie danced and purred beneath. Her mother had made the
journey to communicate with her and the most amazing
emotions of peace and love permeated the awareness and the
hearts of all taking part. Zizie never ran mournfully crying
around the house in search of her mother after that night.
She had found her in the centre of our circle and her grief
had been healed by her mother's adoring spirit.

Moonbeam also came through one day for a client,
Judith, who had never met either her or Zizie whilst they
were on Earth. Judith, an art historian, was also very
mediumistic and was learning to value and develop her gift.
Whilst bringing her some healing I became aware that one of
my spirit cats had joined us and was sitting at Judith's feet. I
asked her to tune in and tell me what she experienced. Judith
described a serene blue-point Siamese, tranquil and loving,
one of mine. I identified Moonbeam and asked Judith to ask
her what she was doing now. She immediately grew larger,
very large indeed, and proudly showed Judith many animals
of all shapes, sizes and species. These were the animals she
was healing, by working with a vet as his helper. She was his
healing guide! She told Judith that because she went through
to Spirit at such a high vibration, she will not need to
reincarnate as a cat.

I asked Judith to ask her what Zizie was doing now in the
Spirit World. Raising an elegant feline eyebrow and allowing
herself a small sigh, Moonbeam replied, "Playing! She is
playing with the little kittens who die and come through to
us. There is plenty of work to do should she choose, and she
chooses to play by the sea shore. She teaches kittens to play
here in Spirit."

When my great, magical, wondercat friend Zizie

entually died of cancer at a grand old age, I was completely heartbroken. I spent searingly painful days cradling her in my arms as I listened to her gasping for breath, coughing, struggling to stay alive for one more Great Garden Grass Game, still purring as she became weaker and thinner. I was selfish. She must stay alive for me. We loved each other so passionately, unconditionally. She had lit my path into the immense and sensational world of healing.

She was supposed to respond miraculously every time to the energy that flowed through my hands. How could she go! How dare she go! Her home was the verdant lawn which served as her stage, the clematis boughs where she often perched, the garden shed roof which was her command lookout post, her beloved flower beds for her night time dances with doomed frogs, and our duvet, her favourite snuggle-snoring place. She should live here with my husband Nick and me forever. I swore never again to invite any animal into my life. Nobody could replace Zizie.

"I don't believe you," said Nick.

"I don't believe you. You have always lived with a cat," said my mother, the curator of my history.

"We don't believe you," chorused our friends. "The idea of you without a cat—Why, it's just absurd!"

But I did mean it. It was my grief talking, of course. The beautiful old soul had found a place to sit in my heart, and now was eventually leaving me, warning me the night before she ascended, "Ingrid, I've had enough now. I want to leave. Let me go. You must let me go."

Those of you who have been trained by Amelia will be familiar with what it feels like to hear an animal's thoughts within your head, knowing that the voice you hear is not your own voice, the thoughts expressed not your own thoughts. The more practice you have at telepathy, the easier it becomes to distinguish between your own fanciful imaginings and the authentic voice of the animal. When Zizie spoke these words to me, I was resistant to accepting them, though regretfully I knew I must. I had dared to hope that she would rally, miraculously recover, right until the last moment. Now through my stubborn head she was pleading with me to let her die. It was her time. Tearfully and with all the unconditional love my soul could muster, I promised her that the next day I would do as she wished and call the vet. Her last gift to me was to die in her sleep that night. God bless her beautiful soul, I never had to make that dreaded telephone call for her.

Léonie is a delightful woman who shared my love for my little lilac cat. Zizie always responded warmly to her, knowing that they could share passionate moments when Léonie came for her treatments. If we spent too long chatting at the start of the sessions, Zizie would sigh audibly until the time came for Léonie to climb up onto my healing couch and I would start to work with my helpers, creating the bridge over which their healing energy could flow through to the physical dimension. As soon as Léonie was on the couch, Zizie would jump up, purring, to sit sphinx-like, gazing at her from the vantage point of Léonie's stomach. She did this with favoured clients.

The first time that Léonie came for a treatment after Zizie had died, she sat with tears cascading down her face. She had loved my beautiful, geriatric, wayward old kitten-cat and was devastated at her parting. I was unable to comfort her or offer a "professional" response as I too was struggling with my sense of loss of her from my physical life, although I sensed her energy around. I invited Léonie to the healing couch. She climbed on, lay down and then suddenly sat up again with a gasp, moving in a way that people do if they have experienced a surprisingly sudden weight hitting their chest. We greeted Zizie with laughter.

Just like her not to let a mere detail like physical death stop her from taking part as usual in our sessions! There she was, warm, purring and sphinx-like on Léonie's stomach, and it was business as usual. What a fantastic healing of grief happened that day.

Reflection

We human animals as a matter of urgency have to enlarge our awareness of the true nature of existence, or as near as we can get with our present understandings, and realize that we are connected inextricably with the other animals with whom we share this planet. We think of ourselves as the most civilized and advanced of all the animals and proudly believe that only humans are entitled to think, feel and express emotions. Those who find any other concept tricky to take on board should certainly not read any of Cleveland Baxter's work on the emotional reactions of plants, that is for sure. The stiff casing protecting them from their true nature would stand in danger of breaking and blowing their small and inflexible grey brain matter to Kingdom Come.

I am reminded of a lovely story about a frog who, hopping around the rim of the well in which he lived, one day looked down and saw another frog. The newcomer looked rather like he did himself, but there was something intriguing about him, so the well frog called out, "Hello! I've not seen you around my well before. Who are you?"

The second frog looked up and smiled in a friendly response.

"Hello!" he replied. "I'm an ocean frog. I live by the ocean."

"What's an ocean frog? What's an ocean? I've never heard of that before," inquired the well frog.

The ocean frog tried to explain but it was clear that the well frog remained mystified, so he invited him to come home with him and he would show him what the ocean was. They set off on a long journey until suddenly, they hopped over the last sand dune and there was the vast and mighty ocean.

"This," said the ocean frog, with a grand sweep of his paw, "is the ocean. This is where I live."

The well frog thought of his well. He looked at the ocean and ...exploded.

Poor little frog. Luckily that was just a traditional tale,

but there are human folk out there who fear that if they were to open their minds wide enough to let a wider understanding into their lives, they might be in danger of exploding too. Their comfortable certainties about the supremacy of humans certainly would be one of the first ideas to explode.

Amelia teaches us about the parallel lives, thoughts, wisdom and loves of the other creatures in our universe. Let us use her teachings and her courageous voice as our lodestar in the work we all have to do: the emanation of this fundamental awareness to as many well frog-people as can dare to accept the unlimited and eternal vastness of the ocean of Spirit; the compassion to understand and accept our responsible place in the daunting, beautiful, cosmic dance of life.

14 DENIS: LOVE, LIFE AND THE AFTERLIFE
By Debbie Lucas

"Denis knew he was dying and so did I. The love that he passed to me was so immense I could have drowned in it. We both sat in the chair for hours on end, Denis would be nuzzling so hard against my neck and chin that it felt like if he could, he would crawl inside of me in order to show me how much he loved me. These moments went on for hours, they were so intense. As much as it was breaking my heart and his, we just embraced each other. I could tell it was breaking his heart too. It was killing me…and neither of us could do a single thing about it. Time and reality were against us. We couldn't fight it any longer. That day was slowly coming when we would have to give each other up."

My story begins thirteen years ago when one of my friends asked me if I wanted another cat. One of her friend's cats had had kittens. It didn't take much thought on my behalf in saying yes to her, I already had one cat, a two-year-old black short-haired female who went by the name of Whoosh.

And so I went to have a look at them. The mother was half Siamese and had produced a litter of grey cats with tabby markings, except in amongst this litter was one that didn't match. He was black—all black! He stood out to me in more than the obvious ways. He was a boy though and I didn't really want a boy. I wanted and had planned to have another female cat. But someone, something, was saying to me, "Take him. He is the one!" And so I did. It was meant to be.

I brought him home and decided he must be named Denis. There was no other choice of name to be considered so it would be Denis and that was that. I had always, for some bizarre reason unbeknown to me, wanted to have a cat called Denis. Perhaps it was subconsciously something to do with the Dennis the Menace character that I used to love reading when I was a child.

Well, Denis settled in once his initial nervousness had subsided. Whoosh got on great with him and accepted him into our small little family. Denis would go everywhere with me. Once I had picked him up in my arms he was quite contented to stay there forever. I would carry him about the house wherever I would go, doing whatever I had to do. If I were cooking tea, he would sit quite contently in my arm, watching me chop and prepare food one handed and watching me cook and stir whatever was in the saucepan on top of the cooker.

I think it was during this time that we formed that tender bond between each other, one so strong it became like no other bond I'd ever experienced before with anyone or anything. This was one that would be built on the deepest, purest, unique, unconditional love that would be made for just Denis and me.

Within six months of Denis arriving in our house and charming us all, one night Whoosh was late coming home. I thought it was quite strange because she was so good at coming home every night just before I went to bed. I left the kitchen window open for her so she could get in when she came back. The next morning, I looked for her in the house but she was nowhere to be found. I went into the kitchen, and there she was. Out the kitchen window I could see her lying there in the garden. My heart skipped a beat; I knew that she was dead. I rushed out immediately and started to pick her up when I let out a loud scream. As I moved her body I noticed slugs had crawled between her legs. It was disgusting. Not only had she died all alone and laid there all night long, but also suffered the indignity of having slugs crawl all over her and make a nice 'nest' in her warm, dead body. I was horrified for my poor, poor girl. I don't know what happened that fateful night and to this day I'll never know, but I had lost a very special, sweet, loving girl who was taken from me far far too early.

Denis helped me heal from my grief. His constant companionship and the love he gave so freely helped me recover and get me through the bad times. I sought solace in him and he gave it to me. Our bond would grow and grow; our love was now so enormous I was surprised the world was big enough to accommodate it!

As time went by Denis grew up into a remarkable young man—a friend and a soul mate for me. We shared everything, all of life's ups and downs, the good times and the bad times. He was there for me, a constant joy, and a constant companion. He developed some strange tastes in food like his passion for peas and his craving for curries. He worked out how to open the fridge door. If he stuck his claws in the rubber seal and pulled hard enough, sure enough the door would open. He discovered that if his Mum was stupid enough to leave a loaf of bread out on the worktop, then I was asking for it to have the corners chewed off, leaving big holes in the polythene or paper bag. If I were stupid enough to leave a bin bag in the kitchen overnight and not put it out for the bin men, then of course I would find the contents strewn all over the kitchen floor!

I was sharing a house with a girl at that particular time and she would constantly tell me Denis kept opening the fridge door after whatever meat she had put in there. If she were cooking, she had to lock the kitchen door to keep Denis out and he would just sit there making no end of noise demanding to be let in! As much as she liked him, I think she found it impossible to cook when he was around. I don't eat meat so whenever she brought meat into the house he knew about it. He could smell it a mile off and it never failed to arouse that frenzy in him. Of course I found all this to be quite amusing. My Denis had become a menace. How cute!

We moved a couple of times in quite a short space of time, but as much as Denis hated it, after a while he would settle to the new house. My human partner had a new job and would be spending four months abroad at a time, so it was just Denis and me on our own.

One winter, we lived in a house that had no central heating and was so cold, the only source of warmth was a gas fire in one single room. If we had to leave that room, we quickly hurried back to the warmth before too long. We had some wonderful moments in that cold house because this was where Denis was to develop more of his endless cheek and charm. I'd be lying in bed huddled up under the duvet when Denis would jump on my pillow. He would stand there purring at me and then start gently nuzzling me with his nose. I knew what he was asking, "Let me in! It's freezing out here." If the nuzzling didn't work, then it was on to stage two of his charm offensive, and this one was always guaranteed to work without fail –the gentle lick on the nose that lay exposed from beneath the duvet! How could I resist that gentle, rasping little lick?

"Come on then. In you come," I would say and he would climb under the duvet and settle down, his warm little body snuggled next to mine and his head resting on the pillow. In the morning the first thing each of us would see would be each other's faces looking lovingly back at one another. I could not find a better way to start each morning. It was such bliss. It also made it very difficult for us to get up in the morning, neither of us wanting to leave the warmth of the bed and each other, to be plunged into the arctic temperatures outside the confines of the duvet. I loved that winter in that house for giving us those special moments.

A few years down the line came another new house—one finally of our own and life was quite settled. Denis didn't really like changes in his life. He used to hate my moving the furniture around and made sure he voiced his disapproval of it. I think that was because he had that bit of Siamese in him, and boy, could he make some noise if he wanted to. We used to have many conversations where he would keep meowing back at me, answering me. It was like we really were talking to each other and he really understood what I was saying, so much so that if I had anything to say about Denis that I didn't want him to hear, I would make sure he wasn't in the same room or in ear shot.

Denis always knew when I would be going on holiday. He would show me how upset he was for about a week before I was due to go. He just refused to speak to me. He would brush me off when I had to say my goodbyes to him and then he would just plain sulk. I hated leaving him and this always made things even more upsetting, and I always missed him and worried about him. He would always go to a friend's house, hang about with the local cats, have a lap to sit on by the warm cozy fire of a night and generally have quite a nice holiday himself. When I came back I would be so excited to see him, I couldn't wait to get hold of him to give him a big kiss and cuddle, but oh no! He would just shrug me off as if to say, "Huh, you are back then?" and just walk off. Did he make me pay! My attempts at giving him cuddles were met with his nonresponsiveness until finally he would forgive me for leaving him and we would have a proper cuddle where he wasn't struggling to get down and away from me.

It was in this house that Denis made the most laughable, cheekiest memory that I have of him. This house was a typical British house with the back garden backing onto another garden and then the neighbor's house. One bright sunny morning I had the back door open, letting in the warm sunlight flood in. Denis had gone out, off down the garden for a stroll as he often did. When Denis returned a short while later, he was calmly walking up the garden path with what looked like something quite large, in comparison to his body, and it was pink in colour. I struggled to see what exactly he had in his mouth. Initially all sorts of things went through my head in trying to work out what it was or should I say what it wasn't—it wasn't a mouse, it wasn't a bird, it wasn't a rabbit, it wasn't a frog.

As he got closer and climbed the steps to the back of the house, I could see exactly what it was. He carefully placed them on the floor in front of my feet and proudly looked up to me as if to say, "Look what I have got for you, Mum!" Two perfectly presented, perfectly clean, ready to cook, slices of bacon! I couldn't believe it. All I could imagine was that someone in the house at the bottom of the garden had had their kitchen door open like me, got out two slices of bacon for their breakfast, mistakenly left them unattended on the worktop for a couple of minutes only to return to find them disappeared, completely vanished out of sight! I could just imagine the puzzled look on their faces, searching everywhere, questioning themselves as to whether they really had actually got them out of the fridge. Oh, and Denis was so proud of what he had done, what he had managed to achieve, and of course we had to let him enjoy his rashers of bacon for breakfast. And that really does give a whole new meaning to the saying "bringing home the bacon!" I still laugh at that little memory and the cheekiness of it; only Denis would do something like that and get away with it. That's my boy!

It was in this house that our lives would change. They would change forever and our relationship would change, and not for the better, and it pains me to think about that time in our lives. I didn't have to tell Denis anything. He already knew the consequences and he knew how things would change for him. Mum was going to have a baby. Denis wouldn't be my baby anymore, he wouldn't be as important and he would be second best.

One day we had been out shopping for things for the new little life that was due very shortly; we had been busily buying all those essential things that you need, wanting everything to be just right for when the time came.

My husband and I came home with the car full of things ready for the new baby and I can remember us both walking in through the front door carrying in the brand new carry cot we had just bought. As usual Denis was there waiting by the front door ready to greet us, but he took one look at the carry cot thinking that the baby was in there and I've never seen him run as fast as that in all my life. I'm sure he was thinking, "You never told me you were bringing 'it' home today." I had to go find him to tell him it was only the cot, that the baby wasn't in it, and that it was safe to come back out of hiding!

Looking back, I can understand how scared he was and rightly so; that unique bond that we had would change. I didn't stop loving him any less, but I knew that the day we brought the baby home someone else would be demanding all my time, time that I would have normally spent with Denis. I knew Denis hated children and babies. If there were ever any in the house, he would be nowhere to be seen and only return when they had gone. I hoped Denis would get used to the situation and after the arrival of our daughter, he slowly did, but something had undeniably changed.

I tried as hard as I could to give my time to Denis and show just how much I still loved him, that I still had room in my heart for him and always would, and despite how much of my time was taken away, I still tried to show him how special he was to me. We did, almost unnoticeably drift apart. We still had our cuddles—our quiet moments together—but not as many as we had had in the past. Before my daughter was born, whenever I used to sit down whether it be for two minutes, ten minutes, or half an hour, sure as you knew it, Denis would be there jumping on my lap ready for some strokes and cuddles. I just didn't physically have time anymore. The amount of times I had to say, "I'm sorry Denis I've got to go and do..." were becoming the norm. In the end he stopped even trying to snatch the odd minute with me. Life was too hectic and busy and he realized that there was no point even trying anymore.

And so our relationship changed. Denis became less reliant on me and gradually there became a distance between us. As hard as I tried to show him my love, he knew things had changed and almost gave up on me completely. If I tried to pick him up to put him on my lap, he just wouldn't be interested and would get up and climb off. We still had cuddles and he'd still give me little licks on the nose the way he used to, which I liked to call our Eskimo kisses, but never that constant wanting to be with me all the time like we used to in the past. This was our new relationship and this is how things would be from now on.

We were only in this house for six months before we decided to move again, this time to a big house in the country, the sort of house that dreams are made of. It had land, it had an orchard, it was in a quiet location, and Denis would love it.

The day of the move, almost everything was packed ready to go, we gave Denis the tranquilizers that the vet had prescribed as he has a terrible time with car rides and because the house was quite a long way away. When it was time to leave, the tranquilizers hadn't done anything and Denis was still acting as normal. He didn't seem the slightest bit subdued. The vet did say to give half a tablet first and then give the other half if need be, if it hadn't worked. We gave Denis the other half of the tablet and by the time the very last bits were packed he seemed to be subdued enough to start the journey. Denis never made a sound through the whole journey which was most unusual for him. Normally he never shuts up!

We arrived at the house and took Denis inside to the conservatory so we could let him out of the pet carrier and have a walk about a bit whilst we brought all the furniture and boxes in. Well the poor little boy could hardly stand, he was still under the effects of the tranquilizers but was adamant that he was going to walk about and explore. He was swaying all over the place and holding his tail out in a perfectly straight line behind him in order to get some balance but he just kept swaying to and fro and falling over! The poor little mite. As much as I kept telling him to have a lay down, he just kept trying to walk. The tranquilizers took ages to wear off; even really late past midnight he would still lose his balance, wobble and fall over. The next day he was fine and able to fully explore without any mishaps.

This house proved to be the best ever for Denis. He loved it—so much space to explore! Fields galore and hardly any traffic about! It was a cat's paradise. All was well in the camp until one evening Denis came home limping. I checked him over but apart from the limp I could find no other damage to him at all so I assumed he had just hurt his leg. We would have to see how he got on over the next day or so. But the next day things took a turn for the worse. He was still limping but as he tried to jump up onto the office desk, almost in mid jump, he fell on to the floor and started shaking uncontrollably. I just held him and tried to tell him everything was okay but I have never been so scared in all my life. I had no idea what was happening and didn't know what to do. This happened two more times in short succession, and I thought that Denis was actually having epileptic fits.

I wasn't sure because I had never seen anything like this. It was just so scary. We took Denis to the vet's where the trainee vet told us he was having muscle spasms due to the injury in his leg and she reluctantly sent us away with some tablets. No sooner had we got back than Denis started fitting again, but with each episode they were getting worse and lasting longer. On the last fit I was so terrified that he was going to die that we just rushed straight back up to the vet's. The vet then said he suspected a head injury and the impact being with something hard and blunt. They would keep Denis in and start him on steroids to reduce swelling to the head and brain and I was advised to ring back in the morning.

The following morning was filled with bad news. Denis had gone blind over night and it was touch and go as to whether he would pull through. My heart sank, I was truly helpless and powerless to do anything except wait, hope and pray. I rang again in the evening and there had been no improvement and was told to ring back in the morning. Denis has always been a fighter through and through, I prayed that he was still fighting; I prayed that he wouldn't give up. I wasn't ready to lose him.

The next morning there had been a slight improvement and by tea time it was starting to look like he might just make it. His eyesight had returned and the vet was certain that the swelling on the brain was subsiding. I was overjoyed. They said if he continued to improve then they would only keep him in for one more day and then he would be able to come home to convalesce.

When we brought Denis home, it was such a joy to have him back here. He was to keep on the steroids for another two weeks. Denis still couldn't use his front leg, in fact it was worse than ever and he was still extremely fragile. He had lost a lot of his balance and control due to the swelling on his brain and I had to make sure he didn't fall over and hurt himself and do anymore damage to his head.

We both camped out in the spare room where I could provide him with the constant care that he needed. If he needed to eat, I helped him. If he needed to pee I helped him. If he needed to move I helped him. Whatever time of night or day it was, I was there, whenever or however he needed me. We stayed together for a week until Denis started to improve and could walk on his own, and feed on his own. After two long weeks his leg started to make good improvement too.

Denis loved my looking after him and spending all my time with him, sleeping with him and eating with him so our bond started once again to reach new heights. I think I was able to show him how much I did love him and how much I always have.

A few years passed by. The grey hairs on Denis had multiplied and gradually he had reached twelve years old. I used to look at him and think, "You are getting old, my man. Look at all that grey hair around your whiskers!" He had slowed down a bit and slept a bit more but nothing to worry about—until he started to drink more water than usual.

Denis's condition was stable for a good six months or more when one day there was blood in the front of his eye.

He had started to tentatively put one foot in front of the other as he walked and started to reach out for things first to check the distance before he jumped. He also started to bump into things every now and again. The local vet sent us to the eye specialist who told us that Denis had lost about seventy percent of his eyesight due to toxin build up from renal failure.

Denis certainly didn't let this get in his way. He would still go bounding round the house like there was no tomorrow. Of course, we had to change. We had to make sure there was nothing left on the floor for him to trip over. We used sound to let him know if he was about to bump into anything; we would tap on his food and water bowl to let him know where they were. We had to make sure that we didn't accidentally close any of the doors that were normally left open, otherwise he would crash head first into them! He would still make his way out into the garden and even manage to get himself down to the orchard to his favourite spot for a sleep in the sunshine. We would take down his water bowl and he would happily spend hours there, taking in the sun. And this was how he spent the whole of last summer, quietly enjoying himself.

By the middle of December things took a turn for the worse, Denis slowly started to refuse to eat and it was not a good sign; the vet's confirmed that the toxic levels his blood work were sky high.

I decide to keep him at the vet's and see if he responded to being put on an intravenous drip and given fluids.

After two days, I was so torn apart by leaving Denis there at the vet's that they let me go sit with him. It broke my heart when he wouldn't even turn round to face me. He hated me for leaving him there, he was uncomfortable, the drip hurt and he thought I had abandoned him. I sat with him for about three hours. He hadn't eaten anything since he had been in. I tapped on the bowl of water and he got up and drank nearly a full bowl. I don't think he knew he had a bowl of water and I had forgotten to tell the nurses to tap on his bowl so he would know where it was. I spoke to one of the nurses about his not eating anything (they had left a bowl of sardines for him but he hadn't touched them) so they went off to find some of his kidney diet food that he had been on at home.

When the nurse left the room I said to Denis that if he didn't eat anything then, they wouldn't let him come home until he started to eat properly again. The nurse came back into the room with the new food and I tapped on his food bowl. He slowly got to his feet and ate a little bit of food as if to say, "There, look I'm eating." The nurse was very pleased and surprised. After we saw the vet and discussed everything she agreed that I could take him home the following evening after he spent one more day receiving fluids.

I was so grateful to have him back home, still feeling really positive and hopeful that his condition would improve now that his body had been sufficiently re-hydrated and that he was back in his own calm environment. I was absolutely convinced that we had managed to stabilize his condition and that it was starting to get back under control and before we knew it, Denis would be back to his usual old self.

Monday morning came and Denis refused to eat anything again, but, "Hey, he did eat a lot the day before," I kept telling myself. In the back of my mind I was so, so scared that the vet would be suggesting the dreaded E word. At the vet's I told her of the good day we had had on the Sunday and hoped this was enough to grant us a reprieve, despite his not eating anything that morning. She said that I could take him home and that there was no point in taking any blood samples because all it was going to tell them is that he has chronic renal failure and that the main thing would be to see if he started eating again.

All I did during the rest of the next three days was spend all day with Denis, cuddling him, sleeping on the floor at night. The rest of the world was put on hold, nothing mattered, everything and everyone could wait, because this was Denis' time. I cannot find any adequate words to convey what we shared during these three days. Denis knew he was dying and so did I. The love that he passed to me was so immense I could have drowned in it. We both sat in the chair for hours on end, Denis would be nuzzling so hard against my neck and chin that it felt like if he could, he would crawl inside of me in order to show me how much he loved me. These moments went on for hours, they were so intense. As much as it was breaking my heart and his, we just embraced each other. I could tell it was breaking his heart too. He knew he was going to have to leave. It was killing me. I found it so hard not to cry during these strong and tender moments and I tried so hard to be strong for him, but deep down both of us were crying inside and that was the reality of the situation. He was letting me know he was hurting inside, not physically but mentally.

I thought my heart would just fragment into thousands of tiny little pieces from seeing this and Denis's heart was breaking too at the thought—and neither of us could do a single thing about it. Time and reality were against us, we couldn't fight it any longer. That day was slowly coming when we would have to give each other up.

We continued just sitting in the chair while I told Denis how much I loved him and he showed me how much he loved me with such force and passion it was overwhelming. Never, ever would I have expected that such huge surges of love and emotion were ever possible. I hated to see him so weak, I hated the fact his body was failing him, I hated the fact that there was not one damn thing I could do to change things except to love him with every ounce of my heart and with every fibre of my body. And despite that, I was slowly crumbling inside. There was no way out. I was locked in my own private hell.

Thursday morning slowly arrived. The vet was due to come at 2:30 p.m. He lay by the fire while I had a couple of stiff drinks--otherwise I might just have run away and never come back, because what I had to do just made me sick right down to the pit of my stomach. I went back to Denis, aware that time was slowly ticking. I didn't want to waste another single minute, I had to get myself under control. I had about forty-five minutes left. I picked him up and we sat in our chair. This would be the very last chance for us to immerse each other in that love we had been sharing all his life. We had to say our goodbyes for the very last time.

When the vet came, they took Denis from me. I almost didn't let go. I didn't want to give him up. They taped the catheter into his leg. They told me they knew he was ready to go because he didn't put up a struggle. But he never did. He always trusted me when I took him to the vet's. He knew no harm would come to him if I was there. I would never let that happen. That was the complete trust that he had in me in looking after his wellbeing. They put Denis back on my lap and within two seconds he was gone.

That night we put Denis in the special box that my partner had lovingly made. We all put in letters that we had written to him. I put in a photograph of Denis sprawled out on my lap to take with him so he wouldn't forget me.

We took Denis outside and turned on the Christmas lights especially for him. We each made a wish upon a star for him and we were blessed to see a shooting star.

As Christmas came I curled up a black fluffy cushion cover and placed it in front of the fire as a sign for Denis in case he should look down and think that because it was Christmas I had forgotten him. I put on a brave face during the holiday but I couldn't have cared less if Christmas dinner was burnt to cinders, I was just going through the motions. My grief was put on hold until it was over. It remained locked up for those few days until it could be let free.

The first morning after Denis passed away, I woke up to feel him literally lying on me, in the position he always lay on me—on my chest with his head neatly resting by the side of my face. It was in those seconds between unconsciousness and consciousness. I wasn't properly awake but I immediately became aware of a really warm spot on the side of my face that was just above the duvet. In a split second I immediately knew it was Denis snuggled up to me. It just came to me in a flash, and then I guess in my excitement with this thought registering properly in my brain, I woke up fully. I then suddenly became aware that this sense of presence had disappeared.

The next morning a similar thing happened. Only this time, again not fully conscious, I sensed Denis again. He was beside the bed at my head level, but the exact spot put him in the space between the bed and the bedside cabinet, which would make him actually levitating in thin air. As soon as I realized that he was there, I immediately woke up, half in shock and half in excitement, my brain fully registering what I had sensed and the feeling just disappeared into thin air again.

At this point I didn't know what to think. I had nothing to base these on. It was new unchartered territory for me. Christmas was finally over and my parents returned back home. A few days later I was typing something on the computer with my head full of memories of Denis which were making me start to cry. Out of the corner of my eye, as I glanced around, I caught sight of Denis walking across the hallway. I couldn't explain this, but the feeling was so strong even though the visual sighting was actually quite vague. I immediately thought the connection or signal was getting weaker somehow; it wasn't as intense as the feeling or sense on those first two occasions. Again I questioned myself. How could I have possibly seen him? It was just so quick. It was over in a flash! Did I really see him? I couldn't explain this. I didn't know how to, and this time I was wide awake.

The next time this happened was over a week later. My partner was packing his bags, getting ready to leave to go back to work for a fortnight so I was feeling quite sad. I was sitting in the lounge in the chair and tears started rolling down my face. I had maybe been crying for a few minutes when out of the corner of my eye, I noticed Denis walk into the room. It seemed to be in slow motion. He had walked about a metre into the room before I turned around and fully faced his direction. There was nothing there. He was gone, yet I had just seen him out the corner of my eyes. It just didn't make sense. I definitely saw him, and now suddenly I didn't. I had Denis's photo by my bedside and I used to just talk to him, telling him things like how much I missed him and how upset I was about losing him and how much it hurt me to have to be the one to make that decision to assist him to pass. I had a hard time dealing with the choice of euthanasia. It haunted me, doubts rose, I second guessed my decision; did I do it too soon? Would he have suffered a horrendously painful death if it hadn't been this way? I hated to have that huge responsibility of making that decision for him and I certainly hadn't been prepared for the insurmountable guilt that would yet follow. Although I knew the grief process would be hard and would affect me deeply, I didn't know how badly it was actually going to grip me, let alone how difficult it would be dealing with the guilt as well.

I used to just talk these thoughts through with Denis each night, while gazing at his photo. I also spoke of the visits he had given me, questioning them with him. I said to him one night, in order to strengthen and maintain our connection between our two planes of existence, and to reaffirm that these visits were indeed real, that if it was easy for him and I wasn't asking too much of his capabilities, could he perhaps reach me in my sleep and enter my dreams?

That night, I was just drifting off to sleep when this image appeared from nowhere. Bam! There it was! It was like a still photo from a video clip or a static image, but it was so strong that it woke me up with a start. All these experiences were sending my head into a spin. I wasn't scared but it seemed like I was on some sort of fairground ride and I couldn't get off even if I really wanted to!

I spoke to my Mum later on and my Mum told me that she used to have premonitions when she was younger. I had never known this and now she decided to tell me thirty-seven years later! I had known that she had witnessed a lot of apparitions during my childhood which came from living in a lot of spooky old houses, but never this.

Around this time also, there were some odd things going on in my house. Every time I went into the bathroom, beads would drop onto the floor, this happened repeatedly yet there were no beads actually in the bathroom to start with. I didn't know where they were coming from. There certainly weren't any in the bathroom when I went in, but sure as you would know, every time I was in there a little tiny bead could be heard falling on the floor from out of the thin air. I used to pick it up and think how on earth could that of possibly happen.

I had two more sightings of Denis after that. One day I was down in the orchard. We had just got six new chickens. There was no way I could have ever contemplated getting another cat, but chickens, yes. And they produce eggs! We were really pleased with all our hard work in making the chicken coup and run for them. After a few days they seemed to be settling in well. I was just on my way back up to the house when there he was, standing right near the very spot where he used to lie sunning himself in the previous summer! I was delighted that he had come to check in on us and to check out the new arrivals!

A few days later we had bought a weeping willow to plant in the middle of the front lawn in memory of Denis. It was beautiful, full of furry little catkins. I was kneeling down planting the willow, with some tears falling down my face. Just as I started to lift my head to look up, there was this blinding white light with Denis standing right in the middle of it, no less than a metre away from me. I just shook my head thinking I couldn't have possibly seen what I had just seen. But I had. It was beautiful.

ABOUT THE CONTRIBUTORS

Dr. Bernard S. Siegel is one of the world's most renowned surgeons, a doctor who initiated group therapy to empower cancer patients. He is the New York Times number 1 best-selling author of *Love, Medicine & Miracles, Prescriptions for Living, Peace, Love & Healing and How To Live Between Office Visits, Help Me To Heal and 365 Prescriptions For The Soul.* In 1978 he originated Exceptional Cancer Patients, a specific form of individual and group therapy utilizing patients' drawings, dreams, images and feelings. His latest books include, *Smudge Bunny, Love, Magic & Mud Pies* and *Buddy's Candle,* to help children of all ages in dealing with the loss of a loved one. Learn more about Bernie at: www.BernieSiegelMD.com.

Susan Chernak McElroy's books and tapes are published in 20 countries around the world. Her pioneering work, *Animals as Teachers & Healers* (a NYT bestseller) remains a classic in the genre on the Human-Animal relationship. A survivor of terminal head and neck cancer, Susan is a passionate believer in the healing powers of animals and nature, and in our need to reconnect with these particular and profound wisdoms. Visit her at: susanmcelroy.wordpress.com.

Alan Cohen is a bestselling author of over 20 books including the bestseller, *The Dragon Doesn't Live Here Anymore.* www.alancohen.com

Marc Bekoff has published hundreds of popular essays and 24 books. His essays for Psychology Today can be found at: http://www.psychologytoday.com/blog/animal-emotions. His homepage is: marcbekoff.com and with Jane Goodall: www.ethologicalethics.org, Information on Moon Bear rescue can be found on the following site: www.newscientist.com

Allen and Linda Anderson are award-winning, best-selling authors of a series of fifteen books about the spiritual partnerships between people and animals. They founded the Angel Animals Network (www.angelanimals.net) to use the power of stories to increase love and respect for all life. Their latest book is *A Dog Named Leaf: The Hero from Heaven Who Saved My Life*.

Ingrid J Collins is a Consultant Practitioner Psychologist, a Registered Spiritual Healer, and the director The Soul Therapy Centre. www.soul-therapy.co.uk; ingrid@soul-therapy.co.uk

Kay Pfaltz is a writer and bestselling author of *Lauren's Story: An American Dog in Paris,* and *The Beagle,* a TFH Publication. Kay has been published in *The Missing Peace: The Hidden Power of Our Kinship with Animals, Etudes britannique contemporaines, Bark Magazine* and Bernie Siegel's *A Book of Miracles.* She is a contributing editor for *La Joie,* and writes a monthly wine column for *Blue Ridge Life.*

Marie Mead is the co-author of *Rabbits: Gentle Hearts, Valiant Spirits – Inspirational Stories of Rescue, Triumph, and Joy.* Marie has also written rabbit-related stories and articles for the House Rabbit Society (rabbit.org) and for Bunny Mad, a UK publication. She has been involved in various capacities with animal rescue, advocacy, and education for over twenty years. She has made a home with special-needs rabbits and other animals, all of them rescues.

Sharon Jogerst is a Certified Massage Therapist and a professional Member of the International Association of Animal Massage & Bodywork. Sharonjogerst@yahoo.com.

ABOUT THE EDITOR

Amelia Kinkade is the author of *Straight From the Horse's Mouth: How to Talk to Animals and Get Answers (Crown Books)*, *The Language of Miracles: A Celebrated Psychic Teaches You to Talk to Animals* (New World Library), *The Winged One*, and *Aurora's Secret*. (CreateSpace) She is an international speaker who lectures in the United States, Canada, England, Scotland, Germany, Norway, Spain, France, Switzerland, Austria, and South Africa where she trains animal lovers from all walks of life including doctors and vets. Amelia was featured in *The 100 Top Psychics in America*. (Simon and Schuster)

Her unique abilities have been the focus of hundreds of magazines and newspaper articles world-wide including *The New York Times*, *The Chicago Tribune*, *ABC News*, *The Boston North Shore Sunday*, *The London Sunday News of The World*, *Good Housekeeping*, *Cat Fancy*, *Dog Fancy*, *New Woman* in England, *Bilt de Frau* in Germany, *Annabelle* in Switzerland and the cover of the *Freitseit Kurier* in Vienna. Miss Kinkade has appeared on television programs such as *The View*, *The Other Half*, *The Ellen Degeneres Show*, *Extra*, *VH1*, *Jenny Jones*, *The BBC News*, *London Tonight*, *Carte Blanche* in South Africa, and numerous news broadcasts in the US, Europe, and Australia. She has been heard on over 300 radio programs in the last few years from Memphis to Cape Town, South Africa. A BBC documentary was created around her work with the elephants in the Kruger National Park and a BBC children's programming tour was created for her youngest most open-minded fans.

Amelia's true passion is assisting organizations who rescue tigers, elephants, cheetah, penguins, sharks, lions and rhino; and trouble-shooting problems in sanctuaries that rescue Asian elephants, primates, bears, kangaroos, and countless breeds of exotic as well as domestic animals. In 2002, she was honored to accept invitations to Buckingham Palace to work with the household cavalry of Queen Elizabeth II and to "whisper" with the hunting horses of Prince Charles. Amelia treasures her work with the Olympic horses who competed in the London Olympics in 2013. She leads her magical Sacred Harmony Safaris in Zambia every year to introduce the world to the wild animals of Africa.

www.AmeliaKinkade.com.

Made in the USA
Lexington, KY
03 December 2014